LEAD THOU ME ON

A PORTRAIT OF TITANIC'S HEROINE,
LADY NOËL LESLIE, COUNTESS OF ROTHES

LEAD THOU ME ON

DR. LONA BAILEY

AMBASSADOR INTERNATIONAL
GREENVILLE, SOUTH CAROLINA & BELFAST, NORTHERN IRELAND
www.ambassador-international.com

Lead Thou Me On

A Portrait of Titanic's Heroine, Lady Noël Leslie, Countess of Rothes
©2025 by Dr. Lona Bailey
All rights reserved

ISBN: 978-1-64960-640-2, hard cover
ISBN: 978-1-64960-700-3, paperback
eISBN: 978-1-64960-688-4

Cover Design by Hannah Linder Designs
Interior Typesetting by Dentelle Design
Edited by Valerie C. Coffman

No part of this publication may be reproduced, distributed, or transmitted in any form or by any means, including photocopying, recording, or other electronic or mechanical methods, without the prior written permission of the publisher, except in the case of brief quotations embodied in critical reviews and certain other noncommercial uses permitted by copyright law. For permission requests, contact the publisher using the information below.

Scripture marked KJV taken from the King James Version of the Bible. Public domain.

Ambassador International titles may be purchased in bulk for education, business, fundraising, or sales promotional use. For information, please email sales@emeraldhouse.com.

AMBASSADOR INTERNATIONAL
Emerald House
411 University Ridge, Suite B14
Greenville, SC 29601
United States
www.ambassador-international.com

AMBASSADOR BOOKS
The Mount
2 Woodstock Link
Belfast, BT6 8DD
Northern Ireland, United Kingdom
www.ambassadormedia.co.uk

The colophon is a trademark of Ambassador, a Christian publishing company.

In honor of Noël Leslie, Countess of Rothes, and the thousands who sailed with her on Titanic, *unaware of what disaster would befall them on passage.*

Contents

Foreword   1

CHAPTER ONE
Noël   5

CHAPTER TWO
Titanic   31

CHAPTER THREE
Grip Fast   53

CHAPTER FOUR
Carpathia   85

CHAPTER FIVE
The End of an Era   111

CHAPTER SIX
Later Years and Legacy   131

Epilogue   149

Bibliography 161

About the Author 175

More from Ambassador International 177

"Holiness is an infinite compassion for others. Greatness is to take the common things of life and walk truly among them. Happiness is a great love and much serving."

—Olive Schreiner

Foreword

It is impossible to write or talk about Lady Noël Leslie, Countess of Rothes, outside the context of history's "ship of dreams," *Titanic*; but her story and significance are by no means exclusive to that single life event. Long before Noël became a *Titanic* survivor, and long after, she was a daughter, wife, mother, and champion of society's disadvantaged.

Because her innate courage and perseverance were so dramatically showcased and circulated through the story of *Titanic*, a good portion of this book does detail the disaster. The Countess, however, was much more than a one-time protagonist in the most recognized maritime calamity in all of recent history.

Noël was a unifying, redemptive figure in the chaotic midst of *Titanic* on April 15, 1912, and her story remains even now as a poignant reminder of humble leadership and selfless resolve. In love, she challenged what it meant to be of peerage title while the tides of sociopolitical and economic injustices lapped at the doors of Victorian nationalism.

For all of the discreet crusading Noël did in Britain and Scotland for underprivileged classes, she blatantly put the class system on trial in April of 1912 when she, a sophisticated lady of

# 2 LEAD THOU ME ON

nobility, "scandalously" rolled up her satin sleeves to row a lifeboat of mixed classes and mixed countrymen to safety. Much to the chagrin of her elitist peers, Noël saw humanity not through the bars of the Victorian and Edwardian Era class system but through the indiscriminate eyes of Christ. What a grand contradiction of her era she was.

Her contributions to the world through her philanthropy and graceful social reform efforts go unmatched. Her willingness to step down from her title as countess and crusade on behalf of others was forbidden trailblazing. Noël trained as a nurse for the Red Cross, joined the fight for women's suffrage, and organized dozens of charities all over the world to provide quality food, shelter, clothing, medical, and educational resources for people of all classes and all races.

Despite Noël's legacy of heroism, she has only had scant mention in the media until this full-length biography. In literature, her rescue efforts are mentioned in *The New York Times* bestseller *Lifeboat No. 8: An Untold Tale of Love, Loss, and Surviving the Titanic* and *The Ship of Dreams: The Sinking of the Titanic and the End of the Edwardian Era*. She has been vaguely portrayed in the 1979 television movie *SOS Titanic*, in James Cameron's 1997 film *Titanic*, and in Julian Fellowes' 2012 mini-series *Titanic*. She is also mentioned in Julian Fellowes' hit drama series *Downton Abbey*.

Despite these references, no comprehensive book has been written about Lady Noël Leslie, Countess of Rothes, until now. *Titanic* is a timeless topic of fascination for people all over the world, and the recent tragedy of OceanGate's *Titan* brings up many of the longstanding questions surrounding *Titanic* once again. One of those questions relates to the redemption of the story. In *Titanic*'s catastrophic downfall upon the world's stage in 1912, it is difficult to see glimmers of redemption as the ship of dreams foundered to the bottom of the North Atlantic, taking the lives of thousands with her. "Where is the redemption in a story of such finality?" we may wonder. The Countess of Rothes, however, is one of those unlikely heroines who nobly brought a measure of redemption to the world-famous maritime mayhem of April 15, 1912.

It is similarly impossible to write or talk about Lady Noël Leslie, Countess of Rothes, outside the context of her great faith in Christ Jesus. She was a devout Anglican in allegiance to the Church of England, where she first learned the virtues of Christ during the reign of Queen Victoria. Noël was raised in the Victorian and Edwardian Eras when British imperialism was still in its prime and society was managed by strict gridlocks of division according to one's socioeconomic status, societal standing, and bloodline. Noël pervasively exhibited Christ's love in a way that far exceeded the typical adherence to general religiosity with its pious acts of distant charity. She spent her lifetime using her privilege of nobility to serve others irrespective of gender, class, race, beliefs, or reputation. This obsession she had with love and justice made her a beautiful oddity among her peers of nobility. She let those age-old principles sweep her into the trenches of others' hardships to be of what comfort she could. She became lovingly involved in the ugly, undone details of others' lives when it was the unpopular and almost sacrilegious thing to do according to the norms of her era.

I feel that I have come to know Noël through the research I have conducted on her life, death, and enduring legacy. She was just as human and imperfect as we all are, but her story has inspirational qualities that set it apart and warrant thoughtful consideration. While Noël never fancied accolades for any of her accomplishments, after months of research, I feel justified in telling her story through a lens of great admiration. She led a royally vibrant life carefully calculated toward the betterment of others and, in doing so, left a beautiful, mosaic legacy that is my honor to share.

Even 150 years after her birth, Noël's example is a poignant reminder of the timeless virtues found in living a life that gives others unconditional love, unity, and inexhaustible compassion. May we be lucky enough to find both practical inspiration in her legacy and to find opportunities to apply it in our own worlds today.

—DR. LONA BAILEY

CHAPTER ONE
Noël

"There was a woman in my boat... When I saw the way she was carrying herself and heard the quiet, determined way she spoke to others, I knew she was more of a man than any we had on board."[1]

In the black morning hours of April 15, 1912, amid Iceberg Alley off the coast of Newfoundland, rowed a smattering of lifeboats. The wooden vessels carried huddled groups of frightened, freezing passengers who had spent the night staring through the skeleton of the Edwardian Era class system at their own humanity. Together, nearly seven hundred remnants of *Titanic*'s 2,240 rowed away from the wreckage of what had been a gilded global dream. The frightened, freezing survivors clung to the little wooden vessels with tense, grieving muscles after witnessing the freeze-drownings of hundreds, including that of the grand Edwardian leviathan *Titanic* herself and the era in which she was built.

---

1   Tom Jones, "Heroic Conduct of Women," *Huddersfield Daily Examiner* April 22, 1912, https://www.newspapers.com/image/815475566/?match=1&terms=%22Heroic%20Conduct%20of%20Women%22.

6   LEAD THOU ME ON

Lifeboat Number 8 was steered by a woman named "Noël," who, before the ship began to take on water, was only to be addressed as Lady Noël Leslie, Countess of Rothes. In her fur coat, pearls, and belted life vest, she steered the lifeboat's tiller toward dawn as weary survivors shook shoulder to shoulder from the icy sea's rhythmic currents. Black night pressed in from all sides as the little wooden lifeboats simultaneously rowed away from the vacuum that had swallowed the unsinkable "ship of dreams" and rowed toward more black night. Survivors each held a pocketful of hope that dawn would reveal a means of rescue.

In the blackness, the only thing the passengers could do with their collectively clinched breath was sing. Until they reached the splinterings of dawn, over the icy waves, they sang in unison the old Christian hymn penned by English Cardinal Saint John Henry Newman:

> *Lead, kindly Light, amid th' encircling gloom,*
>
> *Lead Thou me on;*
>
> *The night is dark, and I am far from home,*
>
> *Lead Thou me on;*
>
> *Keep Thou my feet; I do not ask to see*
>
> *The distant scene; one step enough for me.*
>
> *I was not ever thus, nor prayed that Thou*
>
> *Shouldst lead me on;*
>
> *I loved to choose and see my path, but now*
>
> *Lead Thou me on;*

I loved the garish day, and spite of fears,

Pride ruled my will; remember not past years.

So long Thy pow'r has blest me, sure it still

Wilt lead me on,

O'er moor and fen, o'er crag and torrent, till

The night is gone,

And with the morn those angel faces smile,

Which I have loved long since, and lost awhile.[2]

Lucy Noëlle "Noël" Martha Dyer-Edwardes was born on Christmas day in 1878 to Thomas and Clementina (Drummond Villiers) Dyer-Edwardes of London. Noël was born in her family's Kensington townhouse at 15 Kensington Square in the civil parish just west of Central London. The once-communal gardens of the region framed the Dyer-Edwardes' thin-bricked townhouse constructed in Flemish grandeur.[3] British poet Matthew Arnold captured the essence of Noël's birthplace in his 1852 poem, *Lines Written in Kensington Gardens*:

---

2 John Henry Newman, *Lead, Kindly Light*, 1833, Newman University, accessed November 19, 2023, https://www.cardinaljohnhenrynewman.com/lead-kindly-light/.

3 "Lucy Noëlle Martha Dyer-Edwardes," The Peerage, accessed November 7, 2023, https://www.thepeerage.com/p8538.htm#i85377.

LEAD THOU ME ON

In this lone, open glade I lie,

Screen'd by deep boughs on either hand;

And at its end, to stay the eye,

Those black-crown'd, red-boled pine-trees stand!

Birds here make song, each bird has his,

Across the girdling city's hum.

How green under the boughs it is!

How thick the tremulous sheep-cries come!

Sometimes a child will cross the glade

To take his nurse his broken toy;

Sometimes a thrush flit overhead

Deep in her unknown day's employ.

Here at my feet what wonders pass,

What endless, active life is here!

What blowing daisies, fragrant grass!

An air-stirr'd forest, fresh and clear.

Scarce fresher is the mountain-sod

Where the tired angler lies, stretch'd out,

And, eased of basket and of rod,
Counts his day's spoil, the spotted trout.

In the huge world, which roars hard by,
Be others happy if they can!
But in my helpless cradle I
Was breathed on by the rural Pan.

I, on men's impious uproar hurl'd,
Think often, as I hear them rave,
That peace has left the upper world
And now keeps only in the grave.

Yet here is peace for ever new!
When I who watch them am away,
Still all things in this glade go through
The changes of their quiet day.

Then to their happy rest they pass!
The flowers up close, the birds are fed,
The night comes down upon the grass,
The child sleeps warmly in his bed.

10 LEAD THOU ME ON

Calm soul of all things! make it mine

To feel, amid the city's jar,

That there abides a peace of thine,

Man did not make, and cannot mar.

The will to neither strive nor cry,

The power to feel with others give!

Calm, calm me more! nor let me die

Before I have begun to live.[4]

The Dyer-Edwardes were a wealthy and socially esteemed family, with Thomas, a Cambridge graduate, serving as a prominent member of the Gloucestershire Court of Quarter Sessions. He was named high sheriff of the ceremonial county in the 1890s and made his millions through returns on manufacturing investments. Clementina, who reportedly was strikingly beautiful, busied herself with the usual aristocratic teas and corseted galas of the late 1800s. She was a skilled hostess of social acclaim, who often lent her time to charitable efforts despite her own noble British heritage.

The Dyer-Edwardes' only child, Noël, was afforded a life of Victorian splendor with plush mixtures of what England offered in its marbled palaces and in its unbound meadows. She was schooled outside of London's traditional institutions, largely to accommodate the Dyer-Edwardes' frequent travels. In addition to their Kensington

---

[4] Matthew Arnold, "Lines Written in Kensington Gardens," Poetry Foundation, 1852, https://www.poetryfoundation.org/poems/43593/lines-written-in-kensington-gardens.

Square townhouse, they owned a lavish Normandy château and a sprawling country estate in Gloucestershire called Prinknash Park, where Noël enjoyed frolicking on her girlhood adventures through the walled gardens of pear trees that lined the ponds. Thomas' investing and political engagements caused the family of three to make their residential rounds nearly every three months. By all accounts, Noël had a loving and privileged upbringing in the elitists' rhythm of traveling from metropolitan to cosmopolitan living with the changing seasons.

As devout Christians, the Dyer-Edwardes were of the Anglican faith, though Thomas later converted to Catholicism. Roman Catholicism was still a somewhat controversial faith practice in the late 1800s and early 1900s in England, as it fundamentally conflicted with the Church of England. The Catholic emancipation in the United Kingdom had only taken place in 1829, meaning Noël's family was just a few decades out of the anti-Catholic dogma that so pervasively restricted Catholic persons in parliament and universities.[5] Historian Denis Paz says, "Anti-Catholicism was an integral part of what it meant to be Victorian."[6] In Queen Victoria's empire, the Anglican Church was the state church; and English Catholics weren't necessarily commonplace in Britain's upper-class. In echo of the Queen's own tightly-held convictions, the Dyer-Edwardes were dedicated Anglicans with little sympathy for Catholics during Noël's adolescence. Historian Walter Arnstein wrote in his 1996 piece called "Queen Victoria and the Challenge of Roman Catholicism":

---

5   Julia Baird, *Victoria: The Queen: An Intimate Biography of the Woman Who Ruled an Empire* (New York: Random House, 2016), 32.
6   Denis G. Paz, *Popular Anti-Catholicism in Mid-Victorian England* (Stanford: Stanford University Press, 1992), 299.

How were such attitudes reflected in Queen Victoria's public actions toward, and private views about, her Roman Catholic subjects? They constituted, after all, three-quarters of her Irish subjects and an increasingly significant minority of those living in England and Scotland, in Canada and Australia. Most of her biographers are persuaded that the queen "showed a remarkably wide tolerance toward her Roman Catholic subjects." In 1902, the evangelical Walter Walsh felt certain that "Her Majesty never cared for what is termed 'the Romish Controversy,' since all controversy on religious doctrines... seemed rather out of her line." Her more recent biographers agree that—as Victoria declared in 1850—she could not "bear to hear the violent abuse of the Catholic religion."[7]

CLASS SYSTEM

Noël, who was often described as a blue-eyed young lady of allure was brought up under Queen Victoria's rule during which Britain's monarchy was recognized as the world's most powerful empire. Because of her family's close interactions with the sociopolitical climate of the queen's reign, Noël grew up having regular and intimate glimpses of parliament's relationship with the socioeconomic dynamics of Britain's people. When robed decisions were passed down from the throne, Noël was listening at the door, so to speak, and absorbing the process and its effects on the common man. This vantage point gave the young debutante a

---

[7] Walter Arnstein, "Queen Victoria and the Challenge of Roman Catholicism," *The Historian* 58, no. 2 (1996): 296, accessed January 1, 2024, https://www.jstor.org/stable/24452277.

unique understanding of the tedious dance of politics, faith, and human rights, which primed her for a future in advocacy.

The Victorian Era was fraught with hierarchical organization based on the perception of one's class, gender, religion, race, and general reputation. Social acceptance (which was of utmost importance) depended on the delicate balance of all of these personal metrics in addition to an individual's occupation, region (often denoted by dialect), and financial standing. These categorizations produced the infamous class system fostered in part by the social climates of the Victorian and Edwardian Eras. The class system served only as oppressive yokes for the middle and lower classes of the 1800s and 1900s; but for those of bureaucratic blood, this systematic socialization was just as crucial to survival as the potato farmer's next rain.

This systematic socialization hinged on the fabled tradition of "coming out" for what was known as a debutante. By definition, a debutante was a young woman of teenage years, who, after a lifetime of careful (and expensive) training, was deemed ready to enter high society as a lady. This tradition of debutantes coming out was one of the cornerstones of the class system in the United Kingdom and parts of Europe. It eventually migrated to other countries such as America and is still practiced today in various parts of the world as an evolved tribute to the glory of the Victorian Era.

During Noël's early womanhood, however, the preparation for "coming out" was not just a festive tribute like it is today. It was vital to the sociopolitical fabric of the British Empire through the buttressing of the class system itself. The ritual of families and institutions "socially presenting" properly trained and flawlessly polished young ladies was intended to provide upper-class young men with a pool of quality mates from which to choose. These "quality, vetted mates" would theoretically help preserve and further the blue-blood lineage for another generation once the couple wed and reproduced. A young debutante's coming out was a critical point in her life that determined nearly everything about her future. Luckily for Noël, she was well-received by both Britain's aristocratic society at large and potential suitors.

Noël not only came from a choice family of celebrated means and reputation, but she was also bright and spirited with an arresting physical beauty that society columns were always sure to mention. She was slender and polished, exhibiting a natural sway of elegance, whether at a masquerade ball or a polo match. With her pleasant, mild manner and graceful presence, Noël organically adapted to the social mores for young ladies of noble breeding. She became fluent in the arts of Britain's elite in addition to her academic accomplishments. She excelled in equestrian sports, tennis, garden parties, dancing, and dramatic arts. In her teen years, she showed special interest in dramatics and received newspaper mentions for her theatrical undertakings.

At seventeen, Noël was the consummate Victorian Era debutante and was traditionally presented at court. Queen Victoria herself saw young Noël's official "coming out" at Buckingham Palace in 1895 not long before the queen's death in 1901, which issued a new era of British monarchy under Edward VII.[8]

Following her coming out, Noël unanimously became the young lady of choice for many potential male suitors. She incited great

---

[8] Gareth Russell, *The Ship of Dreams: The Sinking of the Titanic and the End of the Edwardian Era* (New York: Atria Books, 2019), 3.

interest from young men and great jealousy from other young ladies. Just as women's suffrage began to emerge in 1897, Noël began her own ascent into the heart of British society. She was very socially and philanthropically active, even during her initial engagements, going far beyond the dedication of most of her peers. Nearly every event she attended prompted hordes of giggles and whispered predictions of who would win the heart of promising Miss Dyer-Edwardes. Noël was careful in her acceptance of courtship offers, however, and disappointed dozens of eligible young men with polite declines. At twenty years old, she met a particular infantry officer named Norman Evelyn Leslie, the 19th Earl of Rothes; and he was terribly hard to ignore. Noël's heart wouldn't allow her to decline his courtship offer nor his subsequent proposal of marriage.

THE EARL

Norman Leslie was born July 13, 1877, in Devonshire, England, to Martin and Georgina Leslie.[9] Though Norman's upbringing had been a traditional British one, he had thick Scottish blood in his veins, described by the upper class as "peasant blood."[10] Norman's great-grandfather was a Devonshire peasant, who could neither read nor write. He worked as a gardener for the 12th Earl of Rothes and fell in love with the earl's eldest daughter, Lady Henrietta Leslie.[11] The two married in secret when she was only sixteen, and the union wasn't

---

9 "Norman Evelyn Leslie, 19th Earl of Rothes," The Peerage, accessed November 7, 2023, https://www.thepeerage.com/p8538.htm#i85377.
10 "Lord Rothes Puts His Estate in Scotland on the Market," *The Washington Post*, July 19, 1919, https://www.newspapers.com/image/31539121/?match=1&terms=%22lord%20rothes%20puts%20his%20estate%20in%20scotland%22.
11 "A Mixed Ancestry," *Pittsburgh Post-Gazette*, March 14, 1900, page 4, https://www.newspapers.com/image/85571192/?match=1&terms=%22Lady%20Henrietta%20Leslie%22.

revealed until Lady Henrietta succeeded to her father's earldom. Imagine the swooning in Devonshire when the earl's gardener suddenly became lord upon his death.

Norman's paternal grandmother, Mary Elizabeth Haworth-Leslie, was the 18th Countess of Rothes, and he succeeded her to the earldom in 1893 when he was only sixteen years old. Just after his eighteenth birthday, Norman was commissioned into the infantry of Devonshire. Just two years into his service with the British Militia, he was promoted to lieutenant but resigned ahead of the Second Boer War in 1899. He was commissioned again in 1911 and was placed in command of the Highland Cyclist Battalion as lieutenant-colonel in tandem with the Black Watch, 3rd Battalion, Royal Regiment of Scotland.[12]

Norman became a celebrated figure throughout Great Britain and Scotland, not only for his title as earl but also for the integrity and charm that made him deserving of it. He also served as Fife's justice of the peace for some time. He was handsome, debonair, and the perfect match for Britain's most eligible young lady. The court overlooked whatever traces of "peasant blood" young Norman may have had in his veins and praised him as the peerage leader of his generation.

When Norman and Noël met at the customary soirée for eligible young people, their chemistry went far beyond the metrics of "good breeding." Even within the confines of Queen Victoria's traditional empire, it was no crime to fall in love. The queen herself had been found guilty of such when she met and married Prince Albert of Saxe-Coburg and Gotha. In her private diary, the iron-fisted British

---

[12] "Norman Evelyn Leslie, 19th Earl of Rothes." The Peerage, accessed November 7, 2023, https://www.thepeerage.com/p8538.htm#i85377.

monarch privately wrote of her great love for Albert after their wedding night in 1840:

> I NEVER, NEVER spent such an evening!!! MY DEAREST DEAREST DEAR Albert... his excessive love & affection gave me feelings of heavenly love & happiness I never could have hoped to have felt before! He clasped me in his arms, & we kissed each other again & again! His beauty, his sweetness & gentleness—really how can I ever be thankful enough to have such a Husband!... to be called by names of tenderness, I have never yet heard used to me before—was bliss beyond belief! Oh! This was the happiest day of my life![13]

Not unlike Queen Victoria and Prince Albert, Norman and Noël made a fine match logistically, but even if they hadn't, their chemistry would have found a way. After a proper courtship, in September of 1899, Norman proposed; and they were married the following spring on Thursday, April 19, 1900, at 2:30 p.m. at the parish church of Kensington St. Mary Abbots.[14] Norman and Noël married in the same church Thomas and Clementina married; Norman was twenty-three and Noël twenty-two. *The Glasgow Herald* described the bride in glowing detail:

> The bride, who was given away by her father, looked very sweet and girlish in a lovely gown of rich white satin, completely veiled in a very costly lace, and with transparent yoke and sleeves of ruched chiffon. Her tulle veil, with lace applique, was worn over a wreath of orange blossom, and she carried a huge bouquet of

---

13 Baird, 145.
14 Russell, *The Ship of Dreams: The Sinking of the Titanic and the End of the Edwardian Era*, 2.

white exotics. Her train of bridesmaids all wore in the Earl's tartan in the form of a sash from the shoulder across their white gowns; whilst their bouquets of crimson carnations and white heather were tied with tartan ribbon.[15]

The couple chose Primrose Day as their wedding day, which commemorated the death of British Prime Minister Benjamin Disraeli, 1st Earl of Beaconsfield, who died on April 19, 1881. Disraeli represented Britain for many years during Noël's childhood, and her father Thomas was a close acquaintance of the conservative statesman. Carnations and primrose adorned St. Mary Abbots in reverent celebration and remembrance. Their reception was held at the Dyer-Edwardes' Kensington home.

Norman and Noël honeymooned on the legendary Isle of Wight, where the queen herself often holidayed. Upon their return to London, Noël was presented at Buckingham Palace as Lady Noël, Countess of Rothes on May 14, 1900. Noël wore a satin heirloom gown adorned with antique Brussels lace and subtly outshone her royal host and hostess themselves. Noël was of modest spirit but always managed to stand out from every crowd with her perfectly chiseled facial features, slender physique, and the elegant poise she naturally exuded. Those society prattlers who had once giggled and whispered predictions of Noël's future husband became awestruck and a bit envious of the shining, esteemed couple who were actually very much in love with each other, contrary to the proverbial unhappy arranged marriages of nobility.

---

15 "Social and Personal," *Glasgow Herald,* April 20, 1900, page 7, https://www.newspapers.com/image/409214828/?match=1&terms=rothes.

Norman and Noël had entered into a hopeful fairytale seemingly high above the oppression and volatility of the early 1900s. For the throngs of unsettled people in the United Kingdom, the earl and countess became Edwardian Era social influencers, whose personal and professional lives were almost of equal significance to parliament's rulings.

THE EARL AND THE COUNTESS OF ROTHES

With the death of Queen Victoria in 1901 came the death of an era. For nearly sixty-seven years, the United Kingdom had known the same monarch who kept a formidable grip on nearly every letter of kingdom policy. Queen Victoria's reign lasted longer than any before her; and with the queen's son, Edward VII, succeeding her, the international sociopolitical climate began to change with industrial development, transatlantic trade, economic growth, and the advancement of technologies such as Marconi's wireless telegraph that spurred competitive efforts across the globe.

When the rigidity of the traditional class system was being threatened by progressive ideologies and the influence of other countries under Edwardian reign, the British people needed pedestal social icons as their mooring amid such change. The Earl and Countess of Rothes were just the right archetypes. The couple represented the traditional romance and enchantment many wanted to cling to in an era of such upheaval. As the turn of the century threatened at the door of Britain's classic culture, Norman and Noël provided a societal balm in the symbolism and distraction, much like news of Hollywood luminaries has provided for Americans for decades.

The newlyweds had more than a few homes from which to choose for their settlement but chose Norman's country house in Paignton, Devonshire, initially. The couple was of increasingly grand interest to the media and public in both Britain and Scotland with mentions of their holidays, charitable involvements, social appearances, and even their consumer activities like when Norman traveled to America in the fall of 1900 to purchase Clydesdales.

On February 8, 1902, twenty-four-year-old Noël gave birth to the Rothes' first child, Malcolm George Leslie, Rothes. News of the earl and countess' tiny new male heir was celebrated in splendor across the United Kingdom among all classes. Like his parents, little blonde-haired Lord Malcolm represented the best of both tradition and progression burgeoning from the Leslie Clan.

The family of three lived in their Devonshire mansion, and Noël flourished in her new role as the tiny Lord Malcolm's mother. Like any noble offspring, Malcolm certainly had governesses; but as the atypical countess, Noël saw to her son's needs more than her staff did. After Malcolm's birth, her maternal instincts began to eclipse the needs of her only child, as she recognized community needs among the children in Devonshire.

A large percentage of Devonshire's population maintained agricultural occupations in the moorland budding with crops of oats, wheat, and potatoes bordered by the red sandstone coasts. The plights of Devon's laborers and farmers strengthened Noël's convictions of an anti-class system during those early years in Devonshire. The policies she overheard while listening at drawing room doors and the effects they had on flesh and blood in the marketplaces bolstered her resolve to empower those who had been categorized beneath her.

Despite Devonshire's official affiliation with the Church of England in the 1500s, in the early 1900s when Noël lived in the ceremonial county, there were still traces of Celtic paganism mixed with Puritanism and John Wesley's Methodism among Devonshire's citizens.

Noël propositioned Devonshire's churches to organize fundraising events for families of low and middle classes who struggled to feed and clothe their children. She not only initiated these efforts but also donated her own money for the many children who ran hungry in tatters through the streets and barley fields of Devonshire. The countess' selfless contributions only furthered the adoration the people of Great Britain had for her. In her nobility, she recognized needs long overlooked by church and state in her new settlement.

LESLIE HOUSE

In 1904, Norman's great uncle, the Hon. George Waldegrave Leslie, died at the age of seventy-nine. Norman was bequeathed his home, Leslie House, in Fife, Scotland; and Noël, excited by the project it presented, began to invest heavily in the home's preservation. Leslie House was the mantelpiece of the Rothes' estate in Leslie, Fife. The estate's sprawling ten thousand acres was home to dozens of tenants on Leslie House's surrounding farmland rented out to Scottish farmers and their families. Despite the chasm in classes, for Lady Rothes, these farmland tenants first became her neighbors and then her extended family.

Since Leslie House's erection in 1667 for John Leslie, the Duke of Rothes, the thirty-seven-room home had undergone countless renovations and redesigns by the time Norman and Noël acquired it.[16] The home had aged since its development, but the polarizing king of Scotland, Charles the Second, had also done considerable damage to the home during his reign in the 1600s.

Not long after Norman and Noël took ownership, *The New-York Tribune* printed a feature on the home's history:

> Originally it formed an immense quadrangle, but three sides were burned in 1768, and it is the fourth wing which forms the mansion, one of the largest in Scotland. It stands on the summit of a hill, with terrace gardens sloping down to the River Levan, and in the village of Leslie, situated on the estate, is the old church mentioned in the ballad of "A County Wedding," written by King James V of Scotland, who described it as "Christ's kirk on the green."[17]

In 1904, Leslie House was in need of additional reparation to turn the residential relic into the opulent and vibrant home it once was for the couple and their firstborn. One of the first things the countess did upon initiating renovations was sell the four-poster bed that the controversial Charles the Second reportedly slept in when he visited Leslie House in 1651.

Leslie House was the cairngorm pendant of Fife's lowlands with its towering three stories of layered limestone showcasing Georgian brilliance. Noël oversaw the intricate refurbishment of

---

16 Nicholas Uglow, Tom Addyman, and John Lowrey, "The Archaeology and Conservation of the Country House: Leslie House and Kinross Home," *Architectural Heritage* XXIII (2012): 164, accessed December 19, 2023. https://www.research.ed.ac.uk/en/publications/the-archaeology-and-conservation-of-the-country-house-leslie-hous.

17 *New-York Tribune*, August 1, 1904, page 7, https://www.newspapers.com/image/468711770/?match=1&terms=%22Originally%20it%20formed%20an%20immense%20quadrangle%22.

the home's interior with welcomes of modern Victorian design and special preservation of the home's longstanding characteristics of the Scottish Reformation. Noël velveted and brassed the four wings of Leslie House with great reverence for Norman's family and for Scottish legacy. She delicately restored the galleries holding portraits and tapestries of the lords and ladies who had walked the drafty halls before she and Norman. While honoring Scottish tradition, traces of her own British heritage undoubtedly bled through, as her visits to Buckingham Palace inspired some of her revival ideas, such as the addition of bay windows. With the countess's touch, Leslie House became brighter and seemed to breathe more freely, its brilliance radiating throughout Scotland.

The grounds of Leslie House were just as renowned and spectacular as the interior, and Noël oversaw their upkeep. Scottish publisher William Blackwood gave a beautiful portrait of the grounds:

> The plantations of Leslie House are remarkably fine. The species that thrive best seem to be ash, elm, common beech, oak, and the silver-fir. The larch does not thrive so well . . . The beech avenue at Leslie House is well worthy of attention; the trees are about 200 years old, several of them measuring 16 feet 8 inches, at 4 feet from the ground.[18]

Leslie House's acreage was nestled in the River Leven Valley in Fife among villages of farming tenants with their flax mills and fields of grain. Though a far cry from her Kensington Square townhouse, Noël fell in love with Fife's parish and parishioners. The picturesque

---

[18] William Blackwood, *The New Statistical Account of Scotland, Volume 10* (Edinburgh: William Blackwood & Sons, 1836), 114.

River Leven managed to seep into Noël's British-born veins, and she forever considered Norman's heritage and home her own.

In tending to neighboring parish tenants, Noël established beloved traditions that shocked British elitists and nourished the Scottish people. When Malcolm was a toddler, Noël began the tradition of including the children of Fife's parish in her Christmas and birthday celebrations. For years, on Christmas Day, she would invite the parish children to Leslie House for gifts and sweets in celebration of Christ's birth more than her own. Whether intentional or not, Noël became the embodiment of the gospel to those families. Those little parish children who waited so wide-eyed to have a few moments of the countess' time, paired with a Christmas gift each year, surely never forgot the reflection of Christ's love they experienced through Leslie House. Save for the example of Christ, it was nearly unheard of for royalty to kneel to the eye-level of a child in kindness.

Noël went beyond the typical once-a-year charitable gestures and became a champion for the cause of working-class mothers. In local factories and flax mills, women were subjected to long, arduous hours with only pennies for pay. With a love for the outdoors and its health benefits, Noël led groups of female workers on a day trip to Edinburgh's beach to not only boost morale but also to give their lungs a few hours of fresh, seaside air after months and years of mill fumes. The fresh air of the sea and of the Countess of Rothes's kindness was an odd but welcomed experience for the Scottish people. For a British woman of such nobility to enter the perspiring experience of the working class for a better understanding of their plight was Christ personified for the people of Scotland. Noël organized and funded in empathic fury to provide food, clean water and milk, clothing, and healthcare initiatives for Fife's underprivileged. What church and state overlooked, the Countess of Rothes tended.

While heralded in Scotland, the society prattlers of England were clutching their pearls in horror at the "scandalous" endeavors of their own Lady Noël. After all, philanthropy was certainly in style; but inviting the lower class into one's estate for Christmas parties and taking seaside trips with factory workers teetered on indecency as far as they were concerned.

Even in the flurry of such regional activism, the Lord and Lady of Rothes only grew in their love for each other and enjoyed stealing away for meadow strolls over Fife, horseback rides through Leslie's wooden gardens, and North Sea cruises in Norman's yacht that Noël herself learned to operate.

On December 16, 1909, thirty-one-year-old Noël gave birth to the Rothes' second child, John Wayland Leslie, Rothes. News of the family's second little lord was just as electric as news of their first. As she did Malcolm, Noël showered John with love and affection. With two sons to tend to, her efforts in meeting community needs were second only to those of her family. After John's birth, Noël began funding initiatives for several Scottish orphanages and volunteered with the Young Men's Christian Association (YMCA) bazaar and the Children's Guild to improve living conditions and future opportunities for her sons' generation.[19]

In echoes of scriptures, Noël penned a poetic piece for the "Silent Hour" column published in *The Central Baptist* in 1910:

---

19   Kathy Kovach, "Two Heroines of the *Titanic*," *Heroes, Heroines, & History*, last modified October 12, 2019, https://www.hhhistory.com/2019/10/two-heroines-of-titanic.html?m=1.

> *Little crosses, little cares,*
>
> *Little things that give us pain,*
>
> *As we bear them ill or well*
>
> *Turn to endless loss or gain.*
>
> *Little trials now may bring*
>
> *Golden lessons to the heart,*
>
> *Which, perhaps, in after years*
>
> *Sterner sorrows must impart.*[20]

Noël served on the board for regional hospital systems as well as the "new" Queen Victoria School near Edinburgh in its 1908 establishment. The institution originally taught children of Scottish military personnel to support the infantry on the frontlines and at home. This was something of great importance for Noël in part because of Norman's own military service.

In 1911, Norman was again commissioned for service as lieutenant-colonel in tandem with the Black Watch.[21] In May 1910, King Edward VII died, and George V ascended the throne.[22] The

---

20 Countess of Rothes, "Silent Hour," *The Central Baptist*, May 12, 1910, https://www.newspapers.com/image/519421509/?match=1&terms=%22silent%20hour%22.
21 "Mr. T. Dyer-Edwardes' Thank-Offering," *The Gloucester Journal*, August 14, 1915, https://www.newspapers.com/image/792520513/?match=1&terms=%22thank-offering%22.
22 "Death of King Edward: World Wide Sorrow," *Shepton Mallet Journal*, May 13, 1910, https://www.newspapers.com/image/806233848/?match=1&terms=%22Death%20of%20King%20Edward%22.

sociopolitical landscape of the United Kingdom hung in delicate balance with the death of another monarch and impending changes nationally and globally under British rule. Murmurings of war loomed as international tensions increased with Germany and the Ottoman Empire. In the face of Britain's monarchical change barely ten years after the previous, many of the British, Scottish, and Irish people channeled their anxieties into preparation efforts should war materialize.

After the June 1911 coronation of King George V and Queen Mary, Noël trained as a nurse with the Red Cross, which was, at the time, still a fairly new initiative. She invested that training into the founding of Leslie, Fife, Scotland's first Red Cross satellite branch. Swiss businessman Henry Dunant founded the Red Cross in 1863 as one of the first waves of organized humanitarian aid through his experience of the bloody Franco-Sardinian and Austrian battles that necessitated impartial mass relief in the aftermath. Britain established its own branch just a year later known as "a national society for aiding sick and wounded soldiers in times of war."[23]

Since 1863, the Red Cross has come to the aid of millions worldwide; but in 1911, Noël's Red Cross efforts in Leslie provided ambulances, emergency medical training for personnel, and the most technologically advanced aid equipment for mass usage. Leslie's local Red Cross Society named their brick-and-mortar precinct "The Countess of Rothes Voluntary Aid Detachment."[24] While Noël's

---

23 "About Us: The Beginning of the Red Cross," *American Red Cross Mississippi*, accessed November 2, 2023, https://www.redcross.org.ms/about-us/beginning-red-cross/.
24 Randy Bryan Bigham, "A Matter of Course: *Titanic*'s Plucky Little Countess," *Encyclopedia-Titanica*, accessed January 10, 2023, https://www.encyclopedia-titanica.org/countess.html.

peers—such as Evelyn Cavendish, Duchess of Devonshire, and Kathleen Wellesley, Duchess of Wellington—certainly dabbled in philanthropy, Noël's Christ-inspired compassion went far beyond the superficial mentions of donations or supplies often found in society columns. Noël was willing to climb into the barracks of other classes, personally assess needs with her own eyes and ears, and then climb back up to her noble platform to disburse the necessary financing and voice to meet those needs.

There may have been whispers about the countess' doings, but she retained her good standing with her British friends and family in attending just as many masquerade balls with her mastery of the minuet, garden parties, teas, and operas as she always had. Newspapers made sure to detail her always-stunning appearance, which usually included gowns of colored chiffon and diamonds adorning her hair. Noël was a devoted hostess to dozens of dignitaries for the Perth Hunt Races, Edinburgh's "Tally Ho Ball," benefit concerts, and the earl's love of driven grouse shooting often with Lieutenant-Colonel Lord Ninian Crichton-Stuart.

Those social events, however, many times served as veiled recruiting opportunities for the expansion of class desegregation for Noël. Contrary to the traditional imperial constructs, her reflection of Christ's love seemed to be the very manifestation of James 2:1-9 (KJV):

> My brethren, have not the faith of our Lord Jesus Christ, the Lord of glory, with respect of persons. For if there come unto your assembly a man with a gold ring, in goodly apparel, and there come in also a poor man in vile raiment; And ye have respect to him that weareth the gay clothing, and say unto him, Sit thou here in a good place; and say to the poor, Stand thou there, or

sit here under my footstool: Are ye not then partial in yourselves, and are become judges of evil thoughts? Hearken, my beloved brethren, Hath not God chosen the poor of this world rich in faith, and heirs of the kingdom which he hath promised to them that love him? But ye have despised the poor. Do not rich men oppress you, and draw you before the judgment seats? Do not they blaspheme that worthy name by the which ye are called? If ye fulfil the royal law according to the scripture, Thou shalt love thy neighbour as thyself, ye do well: But if ye have respect to persons, ye commit sin, and are convinced of the law as transgressors.

ANNIVERSARY CELEBRATION

On April 19, 1912, the Lord and Lady of Rothes would celebrate their twelfth wedding anniversary. Norman had traveled with his friend Sir Curtis Lampson from Liverpool by way of Cunard Line's *Lusitania* to the United States in February of 1912. He had been charged with a mission of governmental research involving the innovative telegraph system and wouldn't be home to Leslie House for their anniversary celebration. He invited Noël to join him in America to celebrate the occasion in a cottage he rented in a Pasadena, California, orange grove he intended to purchase.

The pair traveled the world with the seasons and their dignitary obligations. Except for a respite in 1909 when the countess fell ill for some months before the birth of little Lord John, the Rothes sailed to the far East and far West with only routine navigation hiccups. A balmy Southern California holiday was the perfect way to commemorate the day the two wed and the years of blessedness that had followed. Always traveling with a few of their staff and often family, the earl and the countess were very accustomed to seafaring journeys and distant holidays.

Norman secured passage for Noël; her maid Roberta "Cissy" Maioni; Norman's cousin, Gladys Cherry; and Thomas and Clementina Dyer-Edwardes on a glorious new luxury liner called *Titanic*.

CHAPTER TWO
Titanic

"There is no danger that Titanic will sink. The boat is unsinkable and nothing but inconvenience will be suffered by the passengers."[25]

Sir Samuel Cunard's British shipping line *Cunard* dominated the transatlantic waters with its fleet of steamers from 1840 until the early 1900s. Because *Cunard* had been the gold standard in transport for decades, there was little thought given to the modernization of its liners until British and German competitors began to move into the travel market. *Cunard* was forced to examine the datedness of their more utilitarian ships with their somewhat plain and "slow but steady" reputations. Ocean travel was rapidly expanding through the technological advances of speed capabilities and wireless communication in the early 1900s, pressuring steamship companies like *Cunard* to go beyond their usual deliverables.

Out of innovative travel achievements that improved speed and communication arose the commercial expectation passengers

---

[25] Philip Albright Franklin, *Messenger-Inquirer*, April 4, 2012, https://www.newspapers.com/image/456357308/?match=1&terms=%22There%20is%20no%20danger%20that%20Titanic%20will%20sink%22.

had of opulent travel experiences with efficient voyages and few inconveniences. Though it required a series of loans initially, *Cunard* rose to the occasion of the market and attempted to rebrand in the early 1900s as the fastest and finest of British steamers.

SPEED AND COMMUNICATION

Steam turbine-powered ships had been around since the 1880s thanks to engineer Charles Parsons, but the Industrial Revolution brought the steam turbine sets into mainstream commercial shipping, largely replacing the archaic paddle steam engines and eventually the triple expansion engines. Innovations were undergirded by the delicate balance of safely and efficiently using the tons of coal necessary to fuel the ship while accounting for its weight and speed.

Ships of the early 1900s certainly used propulsion systems beyond wind and sail, but the competitive edge of speed became spotlighted for the shipping industry on the far side of the Industrial Revolution. Efficiency and profitability were focal points of lines such as *Cunard*, which prompted partnerships with Charles Parsons and his engineering team to install the fantastical steam turbine system in their ships. This system guaranteed an average speed of twenty-five knots with one knot the equivalent to one nautical mile per hour. For general comparison, the Kaiser's Cup Transatlantic Race of 1905 boasted of the *Atlantic*'s victory averaging fourteen knots to the watery finish line.[26] The *Atlantic* was a wind and sail vessel but averaged similar speeds as the tramp steamers of the 1890s, even with the triple expansion fuel engines. In short, Parsons' twenty-five

---

26 "Atlantic History," *Schooner-Atlantic*, accessed January 17, 2024, https://www.schooner-atlantic.com/atlantic-history.html.

knots was incredibly speedy for a commercial liner, making Cunard's partnership with Parsons a keen business move to eclipse competitors.

Guglielmo Marconi's technological advancement of wireless transmission earned him the Nobel Prize in physics in 1909 for successfully transmitting the first long-distance signal in 1901. Writer Warren Tute said in his book *Atlantic Conquest*, "Wireless telegraphy was to deprive the sea of its ancient terror of silence," as before its emergence, ships virtually had no way of communicating with the shore or other vessels, save distress flares or the proverbial act of sending out the dove.[27]

The necessity of Marconi's invention for oceanic travel led to the passage of the United States Wireless Ship Act of 1910 under President William Howard Taft.[28] This act, which was the first federal legislative regulation regarding radio communication, required wireless systems and proficient operators for communication aboard steamers. The Wireless Ship Act had little direct effect on *Cunard* by 1910, as their newer vessels boasted of wireless communication long before the mandate, though the act did press Cunard's competitors for the same inclusions in their own vessels, upping the ante for overall market conditions.

WHITE STAR LINE

After the death of his father, Thomas, in 1899, Joseph Bruce Ismay became chairman of *Cunard*'s rapidly rising competitor: the *White*

---

27 Warren Tute, *Atlantic Conquest: The Men and Ships of the Glorious Age of Steam* (Boston: Little Brown Publishers, 1962), 160.
28 "The Story of an Old Timer: Wireless Ship Act," *National Institute of Standards and Technology U.S. Department of Commerce*, accessed December 28, 2023, https://www.nist.gov/pml/nbsnist-radio-stations-story-old-timer/story-old-timer-navy/story-old-timer-wireless-ship-act.

Star Line. Like *Cunard*, *White Star* was also a British shipping company founded in the 1840s; and though the line had nearly as many market victories (and losses) as *Cunard*, *White Star* had historically played second fiddle in the industry and public opinion.

White Star specialized in passenger travel for decades before J. Bruce Ismay assumed control of the line in drawing popularity and credibility in their 1870's release of the *Oceanic*-class ships. *White Star Line* was met with a radiant initial response for their sleek, modern class of sister ships: *Oceanic, Atlantic, Baltic, Republic, Adriatic,* and *Celtic*. Most of the six sisters served the North Atlantic passenger waterways for years, but the *Atlantic* wasn't as fortunate as her sisters in long service. She would become *White Star Line*'s first major seafaring disaster.

In April 1873, the *Atlantic* struck an underwater boulder in approaching Halifax harbor to refuel and the ship sank. Despite being fairly close to the harbor, more than five hundred aboard perished.[29] The inquiry by the Canadian government deemed the accident and subsequent sinking completely unnecessary and placed blame on Captain James Williams for alleged negligence. Besides the unprecedented loss of life in this maritime accident, the *Atlantic* also represented a significant loss for *White Star*'s reputation.[30]

Just after her sinking, papers worldwide printed the forlorn poem *The Lost Atlantic* by Dr. W.D. Brengle as a sentimental tribute to the victims, their families, and the few survivors of the disaster. For the *White Star Line*, however, such public tributes served as tauntings of their muddied reputation:

---

29 "Shipwreck: An Awful Record!" *The Boston Globe*, April 2, 1873, https://www.newspapers.com/image/428970028/?match=1&terms=%22an%20awful%20record%22.
30 Ibid.

A PROUD ship cuts the ocean foam,
Bearing her living cargo home!
A proud ship sinks beneath the wave,
And brave hearts find a watery grave.

The watch at night saw not the land,
Nor breakers rolling high at hand,
Nor unseen rock upon the shore,
Whose mighty sides the vessel bore.

The giant ribs, with anguish bent,
Allow the roaring waters vent,
While loud above the storm cloud high
Arose the agony and the cry.

But yet, amid the rush and wail,
Stout hearts stood forth where gods might quail,
And deeds of heroism then were done
That men thought not beneath the sun.

Insane and crazed with terror, flew
From death and danger worse the crew,

LEAD THOU ME ON

To find no hope, no light, no day,
While ocean held them fast as prey.

But hush and hark! A sound arose,
And louder, louder yet it grows,
It is! It is! The welcome oar
That brings us safely from the shore.

And now the long, gray line will reach
Securely anchored on the beach,
And palsied hands will grasp it tight,
Clinging there for life and light.

Four hundred men this frail means saves;
Five hundred sink beneath the waves.
No fault of thine, Atlantic proud,
Thou art their winding sheet and shroud.

Thy trust thou keep'st with sacred pledge,
While men to thee their fault allege.
A proud ship cut's [sic] the foam no more;
Her crew have found the eternal shore.[31]

---

31 W.D. Brengle, "The Lost 'Atlantic,'" *The Ilfracombe Chronicle & North Devon*

The same poem wouldn't need much modification to fit *White Star Line*'s later, similar disaster in 1912.

In 1902, the International Mercantile Marine Co. (IMM) purchased *White Star Line*; and IMM's financer, American banker John Pierpoint "J.P." Morgan, became its financial backer.[32] With Morgan's investment, *White Star Line* could not only outrun its own losses but also *Cunard*'s successes. The money that was available to *White Star Line* through Morgan's acquisition lit a fire under *Cunard* and its efforts to adapt to and thrive within shifting market conditions.

In 1906, out of *Cunard*'s chairman Lord Inverclyde's initiative, *Cunard* developed the world's first luxury liner sisters: *Lusitania* and *Mauretania*. The commissioning of the two required *Cunard* to take out a $2.6 million loan, as they spared no expense in the design of the two ocean liners sure to make history as the world's largest and most prestigious. The *Lusitania* and *Mauretania* boasted of elevators, wireless capabilities, electricity, and running water for passengers. These state-of-the-art features coupled with the hulking size and speed of the vessels themselves made *Cunard*'s empire gleam at the top with the launch of the sisters. In addition to placing *Cunard* in generally high regard within the market, the creation of these two ships fueled the preexisting tension between *Cunard* and *White Star Line*—a tension that ultimately led to the deaths of thousands and to the fall of Edwardian Era commercialism.

News, June 7, 1873, https://www.newspapers.com/image/797180654/?match=1&terms=%22While%20men%20to%20thee%20their%20fault%20allege%22.

32 Daniel Allen Butler, *Unsinkable* (Boston: Da Capo Press, 2012), 9.

OLYMPIC-CLASS SISTERS

After the 1906 launch of both *Lusitania* and *Mauretania*, Ismay longed to trump *Cunard*'s releases with even larger, faster, and more elegant queen ships that offered more sensationalized amenities than any other seagoing vessels before them, including *Cunard*'s that held the record for speediest passage across the Atlantic.

The competitive dynamics of the Edwardian Era industry kingpins, driven by the sociopolitical climate of the volatile 1910s, were cutthroat, to put it mildly. For industrial leaders like Cunard and Ismay, every personal and professional move they made was driven by the need for power and prestige and the fortune that naturally came along with them. Their images were tightly bound to nationalistic pride and being set apart on the world's stage as having the most and the best in accomplishment. For Britain, it was important to stay ahead of the Germans and the Americans in the global race toward the shipping industry's idea of "world's best."

Not only were *Cunard* and *White Star Line* (along with their few other competitors) trying to outdo each other in their deliverables, but they were also trying to sensationalize their way out of past losses. Both companies had suffered casualties throughout their years of operation and saw shrewd opportunity to "overcome" any past brand defeats in internationally publicized ways.

With Morgan's oversight, Ismay collaborated with Belfast's Lord William James Pirrie on monopolizing transatlantic transport in developing a class of queen ships that had never before been imagined. *Cunard*'s dimensions were expanded to the very edge of realistic possibility. Ismay, upon Pirrie's facilitation, partnered with *White Star*'s most often used shipbuilding company, Harland & Wolff, to develop their almost supernatural response to *Cunard* through the *Olympic*-class line. The designs of Lord Pirrie and his nephew, Thomas Andrews, birthed the gloried line of which *Titanic* was the darling.[33]

Harland & Wolff was, and still is, a British shipbuilding company with satellite construction sites in Belfast, Arnish, Appledore, and Methil. Along with many of *White Star Line*'s full fleet of thirty ships, all three *Olympic*-class sister ships were brought to life by the company in Belfast's shipyard. Panel by panel, Harland & Wolff made history in its meticulous creation of three of the world's most famous ocean liners.

To accommodate building the three, Harland & Wolff constructed new, monstrous slipways before laying the keels for each ship. *Olympic*'s keel was laid on December 16, 1908, in yard number 400, which led to her being called simply "Number 400" until she was given the name *Olympic*, drawn from Greek mythology's "Mount Olympus" as the dwelling place of the gods or the "Heaven" of the divine assembly of Zeus, Hera, Athena, Apollo, Poseidon, Ares, Artemis, Demeter, Aphrodite, Dionysos, Hermes, and Hephaistos. Her divine name represented a divine fortune for *White Star Line* as *Olympic*'s construction cost $7.5 million. In yard number 401 was laid the keel of *Olympic*'s twin sister: *Titanic*.[34]

The younger of the sister ships' name was also drawn from Greek mythology. The Titans were known as the gods before the Olympians' reign birthed by Heaven and Earth (Uranus and Gaea). Like the Olympians, twelve deities made up the Titans. *Titanic* was named accurately for her marvelous reputation as the merging of Heaven and Earth.

---

33 Butler, 9.
34 Russell, *The Ship of Dreams: The Sinking of the Titanic and the End of the Edwardian Era*, 110.

Olympic and *Titanic* were nearly identical in size and appearance in their respective slipways, with each costing over $7.5 million to construct.[35] Today, that amount would be over $200 million. There were undeniable differences in the two sisters, however, that would become more and more evident as they evolved under the direction of Lord Pirrie and his design team.

The main exterior differences in the two ships were their deck designs. *Titanic*'s A Deck was enclosed by windows, whereas *Olympic*'s was open. *Olympic*'s B Deck also had an enclosed promenade for first-class passengers, while *Titanic*'s B Deck featured additional first-class suites. These structural differences were subtle to the layman, but they became imperative in later debunking the conspiracy theory that the two sister ships had, in fact, been switched by *White Star Line* executives to commit insurance fraud.

Both ships used a combination propulsion system with two reciprocating engines and Charles Parsons' steam turbine. After their launches, each ship required a staff of over 150 firemen to man their massive boiler rooms in coal-shoveling around the clock. Each sister required more than six hundred tons of coal a day to steam ahead. At full speed, the ships could average twenty-three knots.[36]

The "practically unsinkable" reputation really began with the ships' bulkheads. Both sisters had sixteen watertight compartments (fifteen bulkheads) running the length of the ships' bellies. They were considered two-compartment ships because theoretically, they could have two watertight compartments completely full of

---

35 "The *Titanic*," *Smithsonian Online*, accessed November 2023, https://www.si.edu/spotlight/titanic#:~:text=The%20Titanic%20was%20a%20White%20Star%20Line%20steamship,Ireland%2C%20at%20a%20reported%20cost%20of%20%247.5%20million.
36 Anna Marie Welsh, *Heroes of the Titanic* (London: Tangerine Press, 2011), 7.

open sea and still remain afloat. The ships were their own lifeboats, *White Star* claimed. Theoretically, the sisters' blueprints showed them to be unsinkable. One claim by *White Star* was that the ship could be dissected into three separate pieces and none would sink.[37]

Titanic was fitted with three funnels or "smokestacks" to release the fumes emitted from her boiler rooms—the fourth funnel was a "dummy" used primarily for aesthetics, though it did help ventilate first-class smoking rooms. Though Germany developed the first four-funneled ship, *SS Kaiser Wilhelm der Grosse*, in 1896, *Cunard*'s ships were the first British four-funneled ships; so *White Star Line* followed suit in making sure their eldest sisters of the *Olympic*-class liners also had four, even if one needed to be a beautiful phony.

BELFAST'S SHIPYARD

Working conditions within the shipyard were arduous with long, draining hours of manual labor. Working-class males from teens to family men struggled against paltry wages, long workdays, and the bitterly intense physical demands the shipyard placed on their shoulders. Construction injuries on such massive projects were perhaps inevitable, but *Titanic* sent eight men to their graves before she ever left her slipway.

Rivet by rivet, *Olympic* and *Titanic* came to life in Belfast's shipyard under the craftsmanship of more than three thousand men assigned to each ship's construction. They worked an average of fifty hours a week from Monday to Saturday at $2 for the entire week's work. On Sundays, many workers brought their families to the yard to see

---

37 Elizabeth Kaye, *Lifeboat No. 8: An Untold Tale of Love, Loss, and Surviving the Titanic* (La Jolla: The Sager Group LLC, 2018), 182.

the slow but steady progress on the vessels. The Irishmen's work was sweaty, bloody, and back-breaking, tediously assembling the world's largest moving objects.

The ships' sizes were unlike anything anyone had ever seen or dreamed to design before. They were each 882 feet long and 175 feet tall. *Titanic*'s anchor required twenty horses just to haul her into place. The sisters proudly rose from their keels by the hands of thousands, with no one knowing just how eternally famous these sisters would be.

Religious and political undercurrents often pitted workers, from executives to riveters, against each other during construction. Along with the Edwardian Era class system's general division of lower, middle, and first classes, Harland & Wolff employees were further divided by Protestant and Catholic beliefs and their political convictions regarding the Home Rule Bill, which aimed to issue self-governance to Ireland.

The bill faced strong opposition from unionists in both Ireland and Britain. Though it eventually passed in 1914, it was ultimately suspended during World War I, which ensued just after its passage. Despite its ultimate failure, the Home Rule Bill remains a vital piece of Ireland's history in its fight for independence and caused considerable friction in Harland & Wolff's shipyards.

With the religious and political bleedovers in Ireland and Britain, Ulster unionists and nationalists were in fierce battles over the religious and economic implications of Home Rule that loomed within parliament. Such implications created chasms among the ranks that trickled down from Lord Pirrie at the top going, nearly overnight, from a staunch unionist to a "turncoat" nationalist as the beginnings of World War I rumbled in the distance. Even the sister ships themselves incited division at times. To Ulster unionists, *Olympic* and *Titanic* were British ships; to nationalists, they were Irish ships. Protests of patriotism often turned violent in the shipyard as the completion dates neared.

LAUNCHES

Just under two years after her keel had been laid, *Olympic* was launched on October 20, 1910. An eyewitness from England's *Derby Daily Telegraph* reported:

> The sun shone brilliantly on this latest enterprise of the White Star Line. Belfast was bathed in sunshine, and the hills to the south of the city seemed to have been brought within a stone's throw of the river Lagan on which Queen's Island—a place of evil notoriety for its fierce faction fights—is situated. The situation of the slipway on which the Olympic stood, was not well chosen from the point of view of spectacular effect. On the one side—in the yard itself—only a limited number of privileged spectators could be accommodated, whilst on the river side towered the sister ship, the *Titanic*, which will not be ready for launching for some months to come. The *Titanic* effectually shut out the view of the *Olympic* from many of the people that thronged the quays across the river, and altogether not more than 10,000 or 15,000 at the outside could have had a view of an event that had rivetted the attention of the whole civilized world.[38]

---

38 "The Launch of the Olympic: The Biggest Ship Afloat," *The Derby Daily Telegraph*, October 21, 1910, https://www.newspapers.com/image/790860002/?terms=%22The%20sun%20shone%20brilliantly%20on%20this%20latest%20enterprise%22.

This wouldn't be the last time *Titanic* elbowed in front of her twin sister on the world's stage. *Olympic* went on to have a long service life from 1911 to 1935, during which she earned the nickname "Old Reliable," which proved a far better legacy than her sister.

The interior fittings for ocean liners came after their exterior finishes; and for a world-famous ship like *Titanic*, inside and outside required the best. Thomas Andrews engaged the expertise of European luxury hotel architects Charles Mewès and Arthus Davis to handle *Titanic*'s delicate, artful internal fittings. For some first-class passengers, Andrews said, the minute details of opulence would be the most important. Drawing from classical Edwardian Era interior designs—including France's Louis XIV, Art Nouveau, and William and Mary styles, Mewès and Davis cultivated an entire interior world unique to the leviathan of luxury. *Titanic*'s signature grand staircase of English oak, her lavish passenger suites, dining rooms, smoking parlors, Turkish baths, and swimming pool were all byproducts of Mewès' and Davis' ingenuity.

Social amenities naturally emerged from the interior plans and provided passengers (mostly first-class) with a live orchestra, an open bar, elaborate multi-course dinner menus, barbers, a gym, a miniature golf course, and squash and racket courts. *White Star Line* had thought of everything in innovative, luxurious detail for its passengers' convenience and enjoyment aboard their ships. In chandeliered grandeur, *Titanic*'s plush interior was the perfect accompaniment to her enormous and majestic exterior.

As the older sister, *Olympic* embarked on her maiden voyage on June 14, 1911, long before *Titanic* was ready for her own. *Olympic* sailed from Southampton, England, to New York City under the command of sea veteran Captain Edward J. Smith in swirls of fanfare for *White Star Line*'s success in bringing fantasy to life through the magnificent watercraft.

After her first sail, the world waited with bated breath for the release of *Olympic*'s little sister, who was rumored to be just as otherworldly in beauty and capability, if not more so. By 1911, the third sister ship in the *Olympic*-class line had been ordered and given the name *Britannic*, also drawn from Greek mythology. *White Star Line*'s *Olympic*-class line of three reflected Homer's Mount Olympus in gilded glory.

On *Olympic*'s fifth voyage on September 20, 1911, she collided with the British Royal Navy cruiser *HMS Hawke* near the Earl and Countess of Rothes' honeymoon location, the Isle of Wight. Again under the command of Captain Smith, *Olympic* abruptly turned while sailing parallel to *Hawke*; and the much smaller ship was sucked under *Olympic*'s hull, causing both considerable damage. Though there were no casualties, the accident was bad press and money lost for *White Star Line*, as public opinion (most likely fueled by *White Star*'s competitors) began to resound with the opinion that *White Star Line*'s leviathans were too big to safely navigate. What began as their competitive edge became their Achilles' heel in the eyes of their customers.

The louder this rhetoric surged, the harder *White Star Line* pushed against it with grandiose reassurances that their ships' unique, hulking characteristics set them apart from others in their safety and viability. Collisions may happen, and damage may occur because of those collisions, they said; but the sinking that other ships were vulnerable to was virtually impossible for the

Olympic-class. If it weren't for her water-tight compartments and sturdy superstructure, *Olympic*'s collision with *Hawke* could have resulted in casualties or sinking. Newspapers around the globe reported that along with no deaths and no injuries as a result of the collision, *Olympic* stayed afloat, despite the gaping hole in her hull from the impact. The aftermath of *Olympic*'s collision with *Hawke* fostered the ideology of *White Star Line*'s "unsinkable ship" that would eternally haunt their legacy.

Much like *Olympic*'s, *Titanic*'s sea tests and inspections were exemplary after the finishing touches were put on her in preparation for her official unveiling to the world. Eleven months after *Olympic*'s maiden voyage, *Titanic* launched on May 31, 1911. *Titanic* gleamed brighter than Ireland's Brookeborough Diamond at 883 feet long and forty-six thousand tons with the capacity to transport over thirty-three hundred passengers.[39] These statistics were compared to *Lusitania*'s 755 feet length at 30,395 tons that could transport around twenty-one hundred passengers.[40] Both in statistics and popularity, *White Star Line* had, indeed, championed over *Cunard* tenfold in delivering the sensationalized sister ships *Olympic*, *Titanic*, and *Britannic*, with *Titanic* being the prime showboat of the three. Throughout *Titanic*'s construction, she received international press coverage. Dubbed variations of "the monarch of the seas," "the floating palace," and "the 45,000-ton sea monster," *Titanic* was infamous before her one-hundred-ton rudder even touched water.

---

39 Russell, *The Ship of Dreams: The Sinking of the Titanic and the End of the Edwardian Era*, 65.
40 Charles E. Lauriat, *The Lusitania's Last Voyage: Being a Narrative of the Torpedoing and Sinking of the R.M.S. Lusitania by a German Submarine off the Irish Coast* (New York: Undersea Publishing, 2020), 34.

DEPARTURE

Eight days before *Titanic* was to set sail on her maiden voyage with a skeleton crew, she completed her sea trials in Belfast Lough to the River Lagan and finally out in the open Irish Sea. The trials took an entire day, but she passed with flying colors on all the usual checkpoints for speed, turning ability, and how quickly she could be brought to a complete stop. If *Titanic* needed to stop on a dime, going full speed, it would take just three minutes to halt her. Surveyor Francis Carruthers from the Board of Trade signed on the dotted line attesting to *Titanic*'s fitness for traveling safely and efficiently, even if she were at maximum capacity with nearly thirty-five hundred passengers. Caruthers granted an "Agreement and Account of Voyages and Crew" that would be valid for one year deeming *Titanic* seaworthy.

Inspections noted the deck inclusion of twenty lifeboats and reportedly only one lifeboat drill before setting off on her maiden voyage. According to *Titanic* historians David Hutchings and Richard de Kerbrech, the sum of twenty consisted of fourteen standard wooden Harland & Wolff lifeboats that held sixty-five people each, four Engelhardt "collapsible" lifeboats (marked A to D) that held forty-seven people each, and two emergency cutters that held forty people each.[41] Sixteen lifeboats were the minimum *Titanic* could legally carry based on the British Board of Trade's regulation. *Titanic*'s original proposal included forty-eight lifeboats that would have supplied plenty of rescue space for all aboard; but with only twenty in tow, she barely met the minimum legal requirement, much to the chagrin of several of Lord Pirrie and Thomas Andrews'

---

41 David Hutchings and Richard de Kerbrech, *RMS Titanic Manual: 1909-1912* (Olympic Class) Owners' Workshop Manual (Minnesota: Zenith Press, 2011), 112.

engineers, who initially insisted on including more for solid, safe practice "just in case." In the end, however, twenty is all she left with. It was with great assertion that Captain Smith gave the following quote to newspapers before the sail of *Titanic*:

> Shipbuilding is such a perfect art nowadays that absolute disaster involving the passengers is inconceivable. Whatever happens, there will be time enough before the vessel sinks to save the life of every person on board. I will go a bit further. I will say that I cannot imagine any condition that would cause the vessel to founder. Modern shipbuilding has gone beyond that![42]

The twenty lifeboats that did make it aboard *Titanic* were housed far below the first-class deck to avoid "spoiling" the scenic view for first-classers and to downplay the subtle warning that lifeboats could potentially even be necessary. After all, she was unsinkable. After the completion of the trials, *Titanic* sailed the 550-mile route to Southampton in official delivery to *White Star Line*, where she would pick up her passengers and domestic crew for her fateful maiden voyage. Captain Herbert Haddock commanded her travel between Belfast and Southampton and would go down in history as the true first captain of the *Titanic*. She sailed mightily into Southampton with throngs of onlookers watching her proud glide into the harbor.

BOARDING

For the nearly three years it took for her construction, *Titanic* had been the talk of the globe as the largest oceanic vessel ever built, and

---

[42] "*Titanic*'s Captain Skipper 40 Years," *Fall River Evening News*, April 16, 1912, https://www.newspapers.com/image/590545495/?match=1&terms=%22Modern%20shipbuilding%20has%20gone%20beyond%20that%22.

hundreds turned out to catch even a glimpse of her first commercial departure. *Titanic* was bound for New York City.

On April 10, 1912, around the noon bell, crowds of hundreds bade the *Titanic* farewell with tearful well-wishes. As she was nudged from Berth 43/4 of the White Star Dock (now Ocean Dock), no one could have known that the thousands of happily waving handkerchiefs were in actuality sending the majestic ship off to her water-grave. Southampton's farewell was the final meeting of Britain and her Titan ship of divinity.

Passengers of all varieties boarded *Titanic* with similar currents of excitement racing in their veins despite their class differences. Certainly, the class system was just as rigid on water as on land; and those aboard were divided by first, second, and third class and mechanical and domestic crews. There were 325 first-class passengers, 202 second-class passengers, 706 third-class passengers, and around nine hundred crew members, totaling approximately twenty-two hundred people.[43]

First-class tickets cost around $4,350 in 1912, which today would be around $135,000. Second-class tickets were $60, which today would be around $1,800; and third-class tickets were approximately $35, which today would be around $1,000.[44] The cost for each class naturally covered passage and quarters but also class-specific amenities and entertainment. Even though third-class passengers were prohibited access to the ship's choice Parisian café and swimming pool, what

---

[43] "How Many People Were on the *Titanic*? Here are Some Numbers," *History on the Net*, accessed October 4, 2023, https://www.historyonthenet.com/how-many-people-were-on-the-titanic.

[44] Jenni Fielding, "How Much was a Ticket on the *Titanic*?" *Cruise Mummy*, Last modified February 20, 2024, https://www.cruisemummy.co.uk/titanic-ticket-prices.

would be considered meager to first-classers was still considered the lap of luxury for those abiding in steerage.

Many of *Titanic*'s first-class passengers were of celebrity status, representing acclaim of various countries. Among first-class travelers were millionaire John Jacob Astor IV; socialite Margaret "Molly" Brown; railroad tycoon John Thayer; co-owner of Macy's Department Store Isidor Straus and his wife Ida; mining magnate Benjamin Guggenheim; Sir Cosmo and Lady Lucy Duff-Gordon; Lady Noël Leslie, Countess of Rothes; *White Star Line* Chairman J. Bruce Ismay; and another design genius behind *Titanic*, Lord Pirrie's nephew, Thomas Andrews. The foremost in fine top hats, furs, and tailored gowns flounced about the gangway hopeful for the journey to the America's Northeastern shore.

Titanic would be remembered for those of notoriety who boarded her and also for those who didn't. Reportedly, at least twenty nameless people were said to have cancelled their plans to board *Titanic* after having terrifyingly vivid dreams of the ship sinking, and thousands of others formed an unofficial "just missed it club" claiming they, too, were among the lucky lot who barely missed boarding the ship. Newspapers printed reports of more than six thousand who joined the fad of claiming to have narrowly missed boarding: "I count it lucky that I didn't have the price to go aboard this year. If all of us who 'just missed it' had got aboard *Titanic*, she would have sunk at the Liverpool dock from the overload," said artist Percival Slathersome.[45]

Among the most notable verified of the "just missed its" were novelist Theodore Dreiser, wireless inventor Guglielmo Marconi,

---

45 Percival Slathersome, "'Just Missed It' Club Might Have Sunk Titanic at Dock," *The Spokane Press*, April 22, 1912, https://www.newspapers.com/image/932287715/?match=1&terms=%22Percival%20Slathersome%22.

candy king Milton Snavely Hershey, multimillionaire Alfred Gwynne Vanderbilt, YMCA executive John R. Mott, Harland & Wolff's own Lord Pirrie, and *White Star Line*'s financial backer J.P. Morgan.

THE *NEW YORK*

Throngs of spectators huddled *Titanic* on tiptoes from the dock as she was pushed from her mooring and began steaming away from her berth. Hinting perhaps at things to come, *Titanic* nearly met with disaster even as she was pulling out of harbor. *The New York Times* reported an eyewitness account:

> The crowd watching from the quay was breathless with excitement. The people climbed into railway trucks to see what was going to happen. As soon as the *New York* broke loose the *Titanic* reversed her engines and in a brief space of time stopped dead and began to back. Then the tugs *Neptune* and *Vulcan* raced at the *New York*, caught her with ropes by the bows and stern, and tried to lug her back to her place. It was difficult to tell the distances, looking broadside on, but there was not much room to spare between the *New York*'s stern and the *Titanic*'s side. However, no one in the uniform was flurried. The Master of the Port with a megaphone stood on the quay issuing orders across the water as calmly as if he were having tea. He had the *New York* pulled back to the quay and there moored securely. Then he let the *Titanic* go on again toward the open water. She had backed right away toward the deep water dock while the *New York* was being tugged about like a naughty child.[46]

---

46 "Titanic in Peril on Leaving Port," *The New York Times* (New York, New York). April 11, 1912, https://www.newspapers.com/image/20639997/?match=1&terms=%22Titanic%20in%20Peril%20on%20Leaving%20Port%22.

LEAD THOU ME ON

As *Titanic* passed her ship-peers *Oceanic* and *New York* in the harbor's waterway, they each quivered with her departure. The suction created by *Titanic*'s mammoth propulsion system threatened *Oceanic* into a swaying fit and snapped *New York*'s mooring lines, nearly causing her to be sucked into *Titanic*'s hull. Thanks to the quick action of *Titanic*'s crew in reversing her propellers and tug staffers in towing the *New York* backward, *Titanic* reengaged forward and cleared the harbor onward.[47]

It was almost an ominous warning that no one but the smaller vessel *New York* had the audacity to warn the hulking showboat. But whatever foretelling was or wasn't present in the near collision, *Titanic* heeded nothing but full speed ahead after the *New York* was snatched back from her determined path. The near-collision caused some onlookers to wonder if *White Star Line*'s vessels were ships of beautiful destruction, and they continued their well-wishes through clenched teeth and crossed fingers. It is believed that as *Titanic* sped off from her near mishap, a self-assured *White Star Line* employee who wasn't the least bit fazed by the incident infamously boasted from the pier that "Not even God himself could sink the ship."[48]

White Star Line planned for *Titanic* to take six days to make the 3,426-mile journey from British dock to American dock. New York City's Pier 59 (Chelsea Piers) would never meet the fabled ship itself; instead, it would only receive her empty lifeboats after the unfathomable struck.

---

47 Ibid.
48 James W. Bancroft, *The Titanic Disaster: Omens, Mysteries, and Misfortunes of the Doomed Liner* (Barnsley: Frontline Books, 2023), 48.

CHAPTER THREE
Grip Fast

"Gin the buckle bide?" Queen Margaret cried.[49]

In Leslie family legend, Norman's ancestor Bartholomew "Bartolf" Leslie served as an honored chamberlain to Queen Margaret Tudor of Scotland in the 1500s. Bartolf would often ride horseback with the queen tucked behind him. She would hold tight to a leather buckled belt around Bartolf's waist as they galloped the chalk grasslands of Wessex.

One day while riding their usual route, they crossed a creek badly swollen from the recent rains. Halfway through the body of water, Bartolf's horse hesitated in a waver; and the queen gasped, fearing a plunge. She cried out to Bartolf, "Gin the buckle bide?" meaning, "Will the buckle hold?" In his determined reply, Bartolf urged her to "grip fast" as he prodded his horse through the stream to safety. Later, he added two additional buckles to his belt for fear of a repeated incident in which the queen might need to "grip fast." Since the allegorical incident, the Leslie family's motto has been "Grip Fast!" with the family crest bearing the symbol of three

---

[49] "The Leslie Story," *Clan Leslie Trust*, accessed January 14, 2024, https://clanleslietrust.org/the-leslie-story.

buckles.[50] Though the Leslie family motto would go on to help save Noël's life, as she and her family made preparations for passage on *Titanic*, "gripping fast" was the last thing on her mind, for what could go wrong on such a ship of splendor?

PASSENGERS

The Devon and Exeter Gazette announced the countess' noteworthy departure aboard the ship of dreams:

"The Countess of Rothes has sailed in the *Titanic* for New York to meet the Earl of Rothes. They will return home in July."[51] Surely, no reader of this bulletin could have ever fathomed the thirty-two-year-old countess rowing for her survival in a lifeboat just three days later.

Noël; her parents; their maid Roberta "Cissy" Maioni; and Norman's cousin, Gladys Cherry, delightedly boarded *Titanic* in Southampton, along with the hundreds of other buzzing passengers and members of the crew. Noël and her family were among the 325 first-class passengers aboard. Thomas and Clementina only planned to travel through to the first port of call, Cherbourg in Northwestern France, to spend the summer in their Normandy home. With their tickets securing passage only to Cherbourg, the Dyer-Edwardes did not have sleeping quarters to see them through to New York City. Noël and Gladys, however, were assigned a cabin next door to Cissy. According to some sources, Noël was assigned cabin C-37, while other sources say she was given either B-77 or C-77.[52] Regardless of the suite's number, from their intricate vanity fittings to their horsehair

---

50 Ibid.
51 "Notes of the Day," *Devon and Exeter Gazette* (Exeter, Devon, England), April 12, 1912, https://www.newspapers.com/image/791439955/?match=1&terms=%22to%20meet%20the%20Earl%20of%20Rothes%22.
52 Kaye, *Lifeboat No. 8: An Untold Tale of Love, Loss, and Surviving the Titanic*, 83.

sofas, first-class quarters were of radiant appeal and the countess undoubtedly inhabited one of the best staterooms available. Hers would have matched the description in the *White Star Line*'s brochure:

> Upon a dark richly carpeted cloth which will further emphasize the delicacy and refinement of the paneling and act as a foil to the light dresses of the ladies, this company will assemble, the apotheosis, surely of ocean-going luxury and comfort. What more appropriate setting than this dignified Jacobean room, redolent of the time when the Pilgrim Fathers set forth from Plymouth on their rude bark to brave the perils of the deep.[53]

Noël and her traveling troop had sailed the seas numerous times without critical incident; and while thrilling to sail on *Titanic*, in terms of danger, they thought no more of sea travel than they did a scenic carriage tour on their Leslie House grounds. With *Titanic*'s size and state-of-the-art amenities, it was assumed not only to be the largest and most luxurious but also the safest. She was called "the queen of the ocean" as *The Fall River Evening News* reported: "The *Titanic* presented the appearance of a great fifteen-story floating palace, splendid and gigantic in every detail built to be the last word in speed, power, size, and equipment. In safety too, it was believed, the last word had been uttered in the construction of the *Titanic*."[54]

Her innovative design, coupled with other fevered rumors of *Titanic*'s indestructibility, caused many to keenly perceive the

---

53 Wyn Craig Wade, *The Titanic: Disaster of the Century* (New York: Skyhorse, 2012), 67.
54 "Sunken Liner $7,500,000 Palace," *The New York Times*, April 16, 1912. https://www.newspapers.com/image/26040649/?match=1&terms=Sunken%20Liner%20%247%2C500%2C000%20Palace.

ship as impervious to error and the elements. Her primary selling point was the "practically unsinkable" catchphrase that so many subconsciously accepted as absolute truth. The world had been bewitched by *White Star Line*'s sensational claims about their latest ship's invincibility and fell victim to *Titanic*'s allure of grandeur. The *White Star Line* had given the world an illustrious vessel of immortality, and to be among the first to travel on her was the experience of a lifetime.

ON BOARD

Though the Countess of Rothes was a favored figure in the United Kingdom, many American notables also regarded her with awe for both her appearance and her title. Those few who didn't know her still turned their heads when she strolled on deck or into the first-class dining hall because of her imperial poise and natural beauty.

Norman's cousin Gladys was reportedly of a different temperament than Noël as a boisterous, single socialite who always made for a lively traveling companion. Cissy was the consummate helpmate for Noël, though in the countess' usual atypical approach, Cissy was treated more like Noël's family member than a servant. Cissy was a young, starry-eyed English girl with romantic ideas about the world. *Titanic*'s shipyard seemed almost larger than her entire home village in Surrey. Like so many other domestic crew aboard, Cissy was enchanted by every detail of the voyage; and some accounts even suggest she found true love on *Titanic*.[55]

Noël had remained close with her parents, despite the distance between Kensington Square and Fife; and they heard murmurings

---

55 Kaye, *Lifeboat No. 8: An Untold Tale of Love, Loss, and Surviving the Titanic*, 137.

of Noël's "alternative lifestyle" in mixing with classes other than her own, even if it was in the spirit of charity. Despite their traditional values, Thomas and Clementina were immensely proud of their only daughter and her tenacity that gave way to the duality of her reputation. Aside from differences in policies, Noël was open to the common man's interpretation of life and appreciated the progressive yet "scandalous" ideas of women's right to vote, worker's rights, and the systematic dismantling of the Old-World class system. To the general population in England, Scotland, and Ireland, Noël was a heroine; but to the upper-class purists, she was a renegade playing fast and loose with her peeress title.

Titanic's second class was made up of middle-class citizens from a variety of countries. Their accommodations on board were a tier down from first class with bunk beds and less ornate cabin fixtures. *Titanic*'s third class was made up of many immigrants and those in the working class, also representing a variety of countries. Third class had very rudimentary accommodations compared to first class; but to many of the third-classers, their quarters were the nicest they had ever seen. Regardless of which class a passenger belonged to, everyone who boarded had dressed in their very best for royal passage and settled in for their six-day trip.

Titanic reached her first stop through the English Channel waters in Cherbourg, France, on the evening of April 10. Thomas and Clementina Dyer-Edwardes disembarked *Titanic*, along with several other passengers at Cherbourg's port, which was around ninety miles from Southampton's departure point. Noël's parents bade a fond farewell to their traveling companions and envied their plans to complete the journey to New York.

For the first few days at sea, the passengers enjoyed a rich holiday in the "queen of the ocean." There was much drinking, dining, and dancing aboard the floating fairy world of Edwardian glamor. The finest of everything was afforded to first-class travelers, and second and third-class passengers enjoyed their own dimensions of highbrow traveling. A second or third-class experience would have been considered abhorrent to most first-class passengers, but Noël would have welcomed the opportunity for a less rigid voyage.

ICEBERG ALLEY

There is a stretch of the Atlantic waters from the Arctic to Newfoundland banks that seamen have long dubbed "Iceberg Alley."[56] These waters average a depth of three thousand miles, and icebergs can extend several hundred feet under the water's surface. The icebergs aren't "grown" in these waters but rather break off from glaciers in and around Greenland. During the spring and summer months, these icy break-offs of various sizes drift south with the wind and tend to gather in "Iceberg Alley," which is especially dangerous territory for ships. Icebergs are nature's great deceivers, as they may appear small and avoidable on the surface. However, they are jagged and sizable just below, which is never good news for a ship's hull, no matter her size. From January until April, in the year of *Titanic*'s maiden voyage, over one thousand icebergs were reportedly documented. April is a peak time in spring when glacier fragments are most likely to drift into shipping lanes—and drift they did.[57]

---

56   "Iceberg Alley: Newfoundland and Labrador," *Atlas Obscura*, last modified June 14, 2019, https://www.atlasobscura.com/places/iceberg-alley.
57   Donald W. Olson, Russell L. Doescher, and Roger W. Sinnott, "Rare

There is some debate on exactly how many warnings of icebergs came in through the wireless, but it is safe to say there were more than enough to prompt slower speed and more alert lookout precautions.

Titanic's state-of-the-art radio room with Marconi's wireless had two operators: twenty-five-year-old John "Jack" George Phillips and twenty-two-year-old Harold Sydney Bride. Both were employed by the British Marconi Company and contracted by *White Star* for the voyage. With a signal range of approximately four hundred miles, radio operators intercepted messages from shore when possible and from other vessels during transit. Most of the messages intercepted by *Titanic* throughout the voyage were of a light, personal nature, serving as electronic postcards to and from passengers on board.

On April 11, however, the radio room began receiving warnings from other ships close to *Titanic*'s coordinates that had encountered heavy ice fields. Iceberg sightings weren't unusual for that time of year and location; and for a veteran sea captain like Smith, they weren't of particular concern.

The weather was about fifty degrees Fahrenheit through most of *Titanic*'s voyage, with moderate sea winds and clear skies. It was fairly typical April seafaring in the Atlantic with fair to chilly open-air conditions but frigid ocean temperatures around thirty-one degrees Fahrenheit as *Titanic* passed through the aftermath of a cold front on her fourth evening at sea.[58]

Surrounding ships steaming through the same waters signaled to *Titanic* again and again with eyewitness accounts of icy conditions

---

Astronomical Confluence: Did the Moon Sink the *Titanic?*" *Sky and Telescope*, April 2012, https://skyandtelescope.org/wp-content/uploads/Titanic+layout.pdf.

58 Walter Lord, *A Night to Remember* (R&W Holt, 1955), 149.

and near mishaps of their own. Among those nearby ships who received similar warnings were *Marengo, Campanello, Pennsylvania, Californian, Mesaba,* and *Titanic's* own older sister *Olympic*. As standard protocol, these warnings were documented by Phillips and Bride for the Captain's review. There are conflicting accounts on the handling of these transmissions, as some say the Captain blatantly refused to heed the warnings, while others say the messages never reached him in the first place due to a backlog.

In *Titanic's* Second Officer Charles Lightoller's autobiography *Titanic and Other Ships,* he said:

> Phillips explained when I said that I did not recollect any *Mesaba* report: 'I just put the message under a paper weight at my elbow, just until I squared up what I was doing before sending it to the Bridge. That delay proved fatal and was the main contributory cause to the loss of that magnificent ship and hundreds of lives. Had I as Officer of the Watch, or the Captain, become aware of the peril lying so close ahead and not instantly slowed down or stopped, we should have been guilty of culpable and criminal negligence.[59]

Regardless of which blending of accounts is true of the warnings, there was only a slight course change to the south and no mechanical modifications such as lowered speed in response to ice pack conditions. *Titanic's* crew allegedly planned to arrive in New York City ahead of schedule so that the ocean queen would beat her own record-setting speed.

---

59 Charles Lightoller, *Titanic and Other Ships* (Oxford: Benediction Classics, 2010), 263.

The legend of *Titanic* striking the iceberg, like many other accounts of her journey's details, is now a composite of various retellings. Generally speaking, this is what happened:

Around 11:40 p.m. on April 14, 1912, four nights into her world-renowned maiden voyage, *Titanic* steamed ahead through the black ice waters off the coast of Newfoundland. She was roughly thirteen hundred miles from her destination of New York City's Pier 59. By all accounts, it was a clear, moonless night. The seas were as smooth as glass. The night was unusually calm and tar black, making it difficult for lookouts to differentiate water from sky.

Titanic had six lookouts among her crew: Frederick Fleet, Reginald Lee, Alfred Evans, George Hogg, George Symons, and Archie Jewell. The men would work in pairs with two hours on and four hours off, round the clock vigilantly commanding the ship's crow's nest looking for visible hazards. Fredrick Fleet and Reginald Lee were stationed in the crow's nest allegedly without binoculars when suddenly Fleet spotted an iceberg on the starboard side. First Officer William Murdoch was on duty at the bridge. Fleet frantically rang the crow's nest bells three times before calling the bridge with directions to steer a hard left to avoid the mass: "Iceberg, right ahead!" At *Titanic*'s relentless speed of twenty-two-and-a-half knots, it was too late.[60]

Based on Fleet's alert, Captain Murdoch ordered the tiller be moved all the way to starboard, away from the mountain of ice, in a "hard-a-port" maneuver and the engines reversed to a stop. These orders took several minutes to go into effect, but they did manage to steer *Titanic*'s bow away from the iceberg, narrowly avoiding a

---

60   Lord, *A Night to Remember*, 11.

head-on collision. For a moment, sure disaster seemed to have been averted as there was a side jolt to the starboard hull. At first, this seemed preferable to the head-on collision just avoided, but what followed the jolt proved otherwise.

By the time *Titanic* collided with the iceberg, most of the ship's passengers had retired to their quarters and were sleeping soundly, though some of the more jovial were still drinking or playing cards. The jolt of the impact woke many, while others later said they felt no more than a slight prod.

The jolt was the first symptom of the traumatic sideswipe of *Titanic*'s starboard hull against the iceberg that loomed below the black surface of the water. That jolt was soon followed by the curious sound of silence from the cut of the engines. Silence may have awakened more than the jolt itself. The sudden stillness and silence of the formerly jetting, noisy vessel was far more concerning. In a matter of moments, the ship's former twenty-two-and-a-half knots became zero; and the engines no longer roared, leaving *Titanic* a motionless, soundless hulk amid frozen black. She was some four hundred miles from Newfoundland surrounded by ice pack.

Noël was among those alerted that something had gone awry. The countess recalled in an interview with *The Washington Post* ten days after the disaster:

> I went to bed at 7:30, and my cousin, Miss Gladys Cherry, who shared my room, also retired. It was bitter cold. I was awakened by a slight jar and then a grating noise. I turned on the light and saw that it was 11:46, and I wondered at the sudden quiet. Gladys had not been awakened, and I called her and asked did she not think it strange that the engines had stopped. As I opened

our cabin door I saw a steward. He said we had struck some ice. Our fur coats over our nightgowns were all the clothes we had. My cousin asked the chief steward if there was any danger, and he answered, "Oh, no, we have just grazed some ice, and it does not amount to anything."
. . . As we hurried along, Lambert Williams came up and explained that the water-tight compartments must surely hold. Just then an officer hurried by. "Will you all get lifebelts on? Dress warmly and come up to A deck."
. . . We dressed as warmly as we could, and went up to A deck. Mr. Brown, the purser, touched his hat as we passed, saying, "It is quite all right; don't hurry!" What a lovely night it was! I stood close to Mrs. Astor. She was waiting under the starboard ports of the library, and her husband got a chair for her. She was quite calm. The last I saw of Col. Astor was when he still stood by his wife, trying to comfort he.[61]

Upon orders from bridge command, the crew hurried to belay all worries and questions about the sudden turbulence. Many inquisitors were told to simply return to their quarters, their sleep, or their merriment as the ship had merely clipped a small iceberg. To most aboard, with *Titanic*'s hulking reputation, an iceberg amounted to a pebble.

One of the most intoxicating aspects of *Titanic*'s story is the plethora of accounts from passengers caught up in the blind arrogance of the era, despite the tragedy that was unfolding around them. Some first-class passengers' responses to the disaster were rooted in the belief that their gilded man-made machines were indestructible

---

61 "Vessel Near *Titanic?*" The Washington Post, April 22, 1912, https://www.newspapers.com/image/28898026/?match=1&terms=%22Miss%20Gladys%20Cherry%22.

representations of their own imperviousness to error and elements. One such account is of a first-class statesman who, upon learning the ship had "clipped" an iceberg, demanded a porter to collect some of the icy shards that had fallen on deck to cool his whiskey glass.

Another similar account was printed in *The Daily Republican* and circulated around the globe:

> To illustrate the placidity with which practically all the men regarded the accident, it is related that four who were in the smoking room playing bridge calmly got up from the table, and after walking on deck and looking over the rail, returned to their game. One of them had left his cigar on the card table and while the three others were gazing out on the sea he remarked that he could not afford to lose his smoke, returned to his cigar and came out again. The three remained only for a few moments on deck. They resumed their game under the impression that the ship had stopped for reasons best known to the commander and not involving any danger to her. The tendency of the whole ship's company, except the men in the engine department who were made aware of the danger by inrushing water, was to make light of and in some instances even to ridicule the thought of danger to so substantial a fabric.[62]

The gaiety of the evening continued for many until the damage to the hull would no longer allow the crew to disguise the incident. Initially, it was easier for the crew to pacify most first-class passengers who inquired about the jolt and sudden stop because they were mostly on top decks above the injured hull and

---

62 "A Sword Thrust out of the Deep," *The Daily Republican* (Rushville, Indiana), April 19, 1912, https://www.newspapers.com/image/549342535/?match=1&terms=%22A%20Sword%20Thrust%20out%20of%20the%20Deep%22.

saw no immediately alarming residuals. Those in second and third class, however, resided down in the belly of the ship; and while they weren't privy to the open-air, "we clipped a little iceberg, no need for alarm" story on the boat deck, many below heard strange hisses just outside their cabin walls. Those strange hisses, they soon learned, were from the gallons of icy ocean water pouring in through the hull's gash to which those sixteen watertight compartments did nothing but help sink the show ship faster than it otherwise would have. Altogether, the gashes in *Titanic*'s side covered an area of three hundred feet from the traumatic meeting with the iceberg; and below deck, she rapidly drank in the ice water of the Atlantic.

THE REALIZATION OF DANGER

Even with all the placating the crew was doing, passengers of all classes began to realize *Titanic* had, in fact, sideswiped an iceberg, but even that realization wasn't enough by itself to alarm the way it perhaps should have. *Titanic*'s reputation was wrapped up in delusions of grandeur. Whether she struck an iceberg or twenty icebergs, many believed no harm would come to her or her passengers.

The crewmen in the boiler rooms, however, knew the horrible reality. At tremendous pressure, water sprayed into the ship's steely innards as the crew below deck scrambled up ladders to escape the rapidly filling boiler rooms. While statesmen in first class were smoking cigars over poker hands, the men in the boiler rooms just feet below were drowning in the open seas that had rushed in. Within minutes, nearly all of *Titanic*'s three hundred below-deck crewmen were lost to the Atlantic's unforgiving waters.

Third-class passengers were the next to realize the terrible truth of what was happening as many horrifically met with ice water up to their knees when they arose from their beds to see what was behind the jolt and halt. From her hull up, *Titanic* was slowly being consumed by the sea she was born to triumph over. The third-class passengers who were able to escape their flooded quarters in an attempt to reach the main deck were met with resistance fostered by the Edwardian Era class system. As the sea lapped at the staircases going above to the upper decks, crew members prohibited most of the 706 third-class passengers, including women and children, from leaving the belly of the ship.

Some speculate this prohibition was exclusively class-related, while others believe because of the logistics of the sinking angle, the crew did not want those in the lower decks to potentially sink the ship faster by rushing the upper decks. Regardless, a great percentage of third-class passengers perished along with the steerage crew. By midnight, *Titanic* was rapidly taking on water, causing an increasingly noticeable lean to the leviathan as the ship's bow was disappearing below the sea's surface.

As news of the situation's severity spread among the throngs aboard, crewmen were instructed by Captain Smith to launch the lifeboats as a precaution. Once most aboard were aware of the imminent danger of *Titanic*'s damage, many broke class rules and unified in panic. Command's initial refusal to acknowledge the crisis wasted valuable time. The hysteria aboard once the crisis had been acknowledged further slowed rescue efforts. It wasn't until 12:05 a.m. on April 15, twenty-five minutes after the initial impact, that Captain Smith gave the orders to have all passengers report to the boat deck for dispatch in lifeboats.

One of the terrible truths *White Star Line* wanted to shield passengers from wasn't necessarily the ship's damage itself but that, in their great vanity, *White Star* had skimped on a few necessities, such as the then-imperative lifeboats. *Titanic* did not hold enough lifeboats to ferry all of her passengers to safety in the event of a ship evacuation. She had enough for maybe half. *White Star* felt that having too many lifeboats would be unsightly for the gleaming new boat deck and might interfere with the first-class passengers' experience of luxury at sea.

In a fumble, the merely eighteen-to-twenty lifeboats were launched with at least one seaman at the helm of each. A standard practice lifeboat drill was scheduled for the morning of the collision; and Captain Smith reportedly canceled it to avoid spoiling the merriment onboard, so the crew and passengers alike were frantic and confused about procedure, causing valuable time to slip away.

Women and children of first class were given priority in the lifeboats, while protests of all kinds intermittently erupted from the terrified crowd, which was made up of people of all classes. Noël, Gladys, and Cissy were among the first to be assisted off the boat deck and into a lifeboat: Lifeboat Number 8. By some accounts, Lifeboat Number 8 was the second to be lowered into the water from the port side. The boat deck was a trembling ten stories above the ocean's surface; and the creaking, jolting davits weren't much comfort as one by one, they were clumsily lowered into the ice water.

Through whispered suspicions that soon turned to frantic shouts, nearly all on board knew they were in the clutches of disaster. As the wick of panic was lit and began to spread quicker than a fire aboard, Morgan Robertson's 1898 novel *Futility* or *The Wreck of the Titan* seemed to turn prophetic in an instant:

> Amid the roar of escaping steam, and the bee-like buzzing of nearly three thousand human voices, raised in agonized screams and callings from within the inclosing walls, and the whistling of air through hundreds of open deadlights as the water, entering the holes of the crushed and riven starboard side, expelled it, the *Titan* moved slowly backward and launched herself into the sea, where she floated low on her side—a dying monster, groaning with her death wound.[63]

Though hysteria during a mass crisis is perhaps inevitable, as cortisol surges through the bloodstreams of everyone facing the same mortal calamity, *Titanic's* orchestra unified in delaying hysterics as long as possible. *Titanic's* eight-man band responded to the ship's sinking in their professional capacities by playing their instruments in solidarity until the very end. Led by bandleader thirty-three-year-old Wallace "Wally" Henry Hartley, all eight men died in the sinking, their instruments with them: William Theodore Ronald Brailey, twenty-four; Roger Marie Bricoux, twenty; John Frederick Preston Clarke, twenty-eight; John Law Hume, twenty-one; Georges Alexandre Krins, twenty-three; Percy Cornelius Taylor, forty; and John Wesley Woodward, thirty-two.[64]

Though there is some debate on exactly which song or songs the band played in their effort to soothe the crowds, *Nearer, My God, to*

---

[63] Morgan Robertson, *The Wreck of the Titan* (Virginia: Wilder Publications, Inc., 1898), 27.
[64] Jack Kopstein, "The Valiant Musicians: Wallace Hartley and the *Titanic* Ship's Orchestra," *World Military Bands: The Heritage of Military Bands*, accessed October 9, 2023, https://archive.ph/20130105160913/http://www.worldmilitarybands.com/the-valiant-musicians.

Thee is generally considered the song that last echoed through the cold night during *Titanic*'s final moments above the ocean's surface. Some survivors recalled hearing *Autumn, Horbury*, or other nameless waltzes popular among the first-class passengers during delicate social affairs like high tea.⁶⁵

The music with violin and cello composition was played as a salve for the panicked throngs, and perhaps there would have been even further tragedy without it as a second-class passenger recalled: "Many brave things were done that night, but none were more brave than those done by men playing minute after minute as the ship settled quietly lower and lower in the sea. The music they played served alike as their own immortal requiem and their right to be recalled on the scrolls of undying fame."⁶⁶

In mass hysteria, passengers expressed their own individual panic in a variety of ways. Some drank; some clawed over others to get into lifeboats; some holed away in their cabins and stoically awaited death. Some broke the rigid rules of the class system and selflessly gave up their would-be seat in a lifeboat, while others tried to piously enforce them in vain. *Titanic*'s infamy had so prematurely resounded around the world in a sort of indestructible tone that some passengers remained in denial to the cold, dark end. Even the countess' own maid, Cissy, said, "I was not at all frightened. Everybody was saying as we left the ship that 'she was good for twelve hours yet' and I was too numb to realize the terror of it all until we were safe on board the *Carpathia*."⁶⁷

---

65 Ibid.
66 Sarah Baumann, "The Musicians of the *Titanic*," *One Day Creative*, April 13, 2021, https://onedaycreative.com/the-musicians-of-the-titanic.
67 "Lady Rothes: The *Titanic*'s Heroine," *Nobility.org*, last modified June 30, 2016, https://nobility.org/2016/06/lady-rothes-titanics-heroine.

No two persons aboard experienced *Titanic*'s slow drowning in the same way, though horror raced through each class with similar screams and strategies of survival. First-class passengers still had a small margin for advantage as most were physically closer to the boat deck's few lifeboats compared to second and third classes and scatters of crewmen.

CQD

Minutes after the collision, Jack Phillips and Harold Bride got on the wireless with distress calls sent to nearby ships with the closest being *Californian* at approximately ten to twenty miles away from *Titanic*'s coordinates. CQD preceded SOS in Morse code, and Phillips tapped out his wireless shouts of help, first with CQD and then the contemporary distress call SOS. With the failure of her water-tight compartments and the lack of lifeboat capacity, the wireless was the only glimmer of a chance *Titanic* had.

Several ships had picked up the *Titanic*'s distress calls, but no one was less than twenty miles away; and there were ice fields to contend with. Several ships did reroute in an effort to respond, including *Carpathia* and *Olympic*; but both were over one hundred miles from *Titanic*'s coordinates and wouldn't be able to reach her in time.

One of the last messages Phillips sent as water rushed the leaning radio room was, "We are putting passengers off in small boats. Women and children in boats. Cannot last much longer. Losing power." After Bride fastened a lifebelt around Phillips, who remained standing at the radio desk, Phillips sent off his last message: "Come quick. Engine room nearly full." And with that, *Titanic*'s wireless went silent at 12:17 a.m.[68]

---

68 Kaye, *Lifeboat No. 8: An Untold Tale of Love, Loss, and Surviving the Titanic*, 455.

Jack Phillips died from hypothermia as *Titanic* was consumed by the freezing sea. Harold Bride was rescued after falling from a lifeboat and counted among the survivors. Bride later said of Phillips:

> I went out on deck and looked around. The water was close up to the boat deck. There was a great scramble aft, and how poor Phillips worked through it I don't know. He was a brave man. I learned to love him that night and I suddenly felt a great reverence for him to see him standing there sticking to his work while everybody else was raging about. I will never live to forget the work of Phillips for the last awful fifteen minutes.[69]

In addition to wireless transmissions, crewmen also shot off distress flares, which *Californian* was reportedly close enough to see, yet ignored as mere celebratory fireworks rather than a last resort SOS. *Titanic* had no viable assistance as she succumbed to her hull injuries save for the phantom light.

PHANTOM LIGHT

When the wireless went silent, responding ships were still miles and miles from *Titanic*'s coordinates. Many, such as *Mount Temple*, were forced to turn back when the icy conditions made it dangerous for them to continue their rescue efforts toward *Titanic*'s location. Many survivors, including the countess, claimed to see the lights of a ship that appeared to be near enough for lifeboats to row out to. Captain Smith also allegedly noticed the light cutting through the black and initially sent lifeboats toward it in a ferrying effort to load

---

69 "Two Heroes in 'Wireless' Room," *The Daily Mirror*, April 20, 1912, https://www.newspapers.com/image/789729135/?match=1&terms=%22I%20went%20out%20on%20deck%20and%20looked%20around%22.

and reload upon connecting with the other mystery vessel. There has been much speculation about the identity of that other ship, as no lifeboat ever reached her mysterious light—it simply vanished as lifeboats rowed closer.

The countess recalled:

> Capt. Smith stood shoulder to shoulder with me as I got into the lifeboat, and his last words were to the lone seaman—Tom Jones—"Row straight for those ship lights over there; leave your passengers on board of her and return as soon as you can." ... As I know something about boats, I took command of the tiller ... Indeed, I saw—we all saw—a ship's light not more than 3 [sic] miles away! For three hours we pulled steadily for the two masthead lights that showed brilliantly in the darkness. For a few minutes we saw the ship's port light, then it vanished, and the masthead lights got dimmer on the horizon until they, too, disappeared. Our boat was the farthest away because we had chased the phantom lights for three hours.[70]

The countess continued:

> Capt. Smith's whole attitude was one of great calmness and courage, and I am sure that he thought that the ship—whose lights we could see plainly—would pick us up and that our lifeboats would be able to do double duty in ferrying passengers to the help that gleamed so near.

---

70 "Vessel Near *Titanic?*" *The Washington Post* (Washington, D.C.), April 22, 1912. https://www.newspapers.com/image/28898026/?match=1&terms=%22Miss%20Gladys%20Cherry%22.

There were two stewards in boat No. 8 with us and 31 women. The name of the steward was Crawford. We were lowered quietly into the water and when we had pushed off from the *Titanic*'s side I asked the seaman if he would care to have me take the tiller, as I knew something about boats. He said, "Certainly, lady." I climbed aft into the stern sheets and asked my cousin to help me.[71]

Based on the Commerce Committee of the United States Senate's inquiry into the disaster, many historians theorize that the mystery ship may have been Norway's seal-hunting ship, *Samson*, the *Californian* could have been closer than they documented, or another ship unaccounted for could have been the source of the light. Another theory suggests the phantom light may have simply been an optical illusion given the visibility conditions of the night.

The countess recalled, "The first impression I had as we left the ship was that above all things we must not lose our self-control. We had no officer to take command of our boat, and the little seaman had to assume all the responsibility. He did it nobly, alternately cheering us with words of encouragement, then rowing doggedly."[72]

After Lifeboat Number 8 was loaded at half capacity, like so many other lifeboats were that evening, Tom Jones took charge of the small vessel as its passengers were clenched in hysterics over leaving their husbands and friends aboard the Edwardian mammoth that was quickly becoming an ice grave to thousands.

---

[71] "Horror of the Chase of the Phantom Light," *The Arkansas Gazette* (Little Rock, Arkansas), April 26, 1912, https://www.newspapers.com/image/138384366/?terms=%22whole%20attitude%20was%20one%20of%20great%20calmness%20and%20courage%22.

[72] Ibid.

There were two or three male crew members aboard Lifeboat Number 8 besides Tom and twenty-five to thirty female passengers.

Among those who left true love behind was Maria Josefa Perez de Soto y Vallejo. Maria was the young wife of Victor de Satode Peñasco y Castellana. The couple was from Madrid and the only first-class Spanish passengers aboard *Titanic*. Victor, like so many other heroic men did for their own wives, escorted Maria into a lifeboat while he stayed stoically behind on deck knowing what watery fate awaited him.

Maria and her maid were seated in the lifeboat just after the countess; and Victor, knowing it would be the last time he and his bride would be together in earthly presence, asked the countess to care for her. She recalled, "Then Signora de Satode Penasco began to scream for her husband. It was too horrible. I left the tiller to my cousin and slipped down beside her to be of what comfort I could. Poor woman! Her sobs tore our hearts and her moans were unspeakable in their sadness. Miss Cherry stayed at the tiller of our boat until the *Carpathia* picked us up."[73]

As Lifeboat Number 8 launched from the leaning deck of *Titanic* around 1 a.m. on April 15, Tom quickly realized he needed a second seaman at the boat's tiller when they hit the water's surface but said the few men aboard were too hysterical and appeared too physically delicate for delegation. Steward Alfred Crawford was also aboard Lifeboat Number 8, but Tom knew it would take more than just Crawford and himself to survive.

Out of the thirty to thirty-five people in Lifeboat Number 8, Tom noticed the impenetrable poise and leadership quality of

---

73   Ibid.

one particular female passenger in the lifeboat: the Countess of Rothes. In surviving the frozen flat waters, she quickly became simply "Noël" to her fellow passengers. Noël busily comforted the others with soothing assurance as their small, wooden savior glided into nothingness.

Able seaman Thomas "Tom" William Jones was born on November 15, 1877, in the Wales village of Cemaes. Tom was born with saltwater in his veins coming from a long line of seamen.[74] After losing both of his parents at an early age, he took to the high seas and grew to consider the ocean his only true love. Tom was a handsome but hardened man when he and the countess crossed paths. At thirty-two years old, he was an expert seaman with robust physicality and endurance for just such occasions as emergency evacuations. Noël was just a year older than Tom; but the seas' weathering made him seem at least ten years her senior, as he commanded their little lot with vigor and intentionality. Tom was almost a member of the "just missed it club," as he had been working aboard the *White Star Line*'s *Oceanic* in April of 1912 as an able seaman. He suddenly asked to transfer to *Titanic* at the last minute just before she sailed from Southampton. Some say Jones' transfer request came about when he caught a dockside glimpse of the beautiful Countess of Rothes boarding *Titanic*. Never could anyone have imagined the two together under such circumstances with Tom at the bow commanding a countess at the tiller as the world's mighty *Titanic* eternally faltered.[75]

---

[74] "Thomas William Jones: RMS *Titanic* Able Seaman," *Encyclopedia-Titanica*, accessed November 14, 2023, https://www.encyclopedia-titanica.org/titanic-survivor/thomas-william-jones.html.

[75] Ibid.

Noël earnestly accepted Tom's appointment at the tiller, even with her nightdress, pearls, and fur coat under her life jacket. Her maid, Cissy, and cousin, Gladys, sat shivering among the lot, as Noël got to work with few instructions on tilling. All lifeboat passengers, including Tom and Noël, were emotionally torn between the chance of light ahead of them as they rowed and the dreadful scene of helpless destruction behind them. Lifeboat Number 8 was the second of all the lifeboats to be dispatched, so the countess' group had dreadful front-row seats for the duration of the sinking. The initial rowing they had done toward the seemingly nearby light put them at an advantageous distance as *Titanic* sunk lower and lower beneath the ocean's surface, as the terrible suction she created was feared to pull anything within close range down with her.

The countess watched in horror as *Titanic*'s electric lights flickered and faded as her bow sunk lower and lower. When her front two funnels had nearly disappeared below the water's surface, her middle split wide open. The weight of the icy seawater flooding *Titanic* deck by deck pulled her into its depths at a rapid speed. Water overtook every inch of ingenuity and every promise of traditional grandeur as *Titanic*'s beautiful fittings were conquered by nature before the very eyes of her passengers, who had been safe aboard her just a few hours before. After *Titanic* split in half from the water weight, the front half of the ship was sucked downward into the abyss as the back half rose almost to a spine-straight stand. The countess recalled:

> The most awful part of the whole thing was seeing the rows of portholes vanishing one by one. Several of us—and Tom Jones—wanted to row back and see

if there was not some chance of rescuing any one that had possibly survived, but the majority in the boat ruled, that we had no right to risk their lives on the bare chance of finding any one alive after the final plunge. They also said that the captain's own orders had been to "row for those ship lights over there," and that we who wished to try for others who might be drowning had no business to interfere with his orders. Of course that settled the matter, and we rowed on.[76]

According to the *Western Daily Press,* the countess later wrote, "The terror of seeing that boat go down, the fearful screams and shrieks of the steerage passengers who were left was too awful. Like an earthquake or a distant battle, the whole ship went under."[77]

Titanic's grand staircase of English oak, her velveted staterooms, her crystal chandeliers, her lofty promenades, and fine bone China dishes were all devoured by the waters of the North Atlantic, while those in scatters of lifeboats watched helplessly. Her champagne bottles and stained-glass domes were shattered and her cargo of prized possessions of her travelers were forever lost. From the heirloom jewels of first-class to the heirloom Bibles of third, from her lavish staterooms to her basic third-class bunkers, *Titanic* was engulfed bow to stern by the watery black, taking with her more than fifteen hundred lives.

Titanic took three years to construct, and it only took her three hours to sink to her death at the bottom of the sea. Over

---

76 "Horror of the Chase of the Phantom Light," The Arkansas Gazette, April 26, 1912, https://www.newspapers.com/image/138384366/?terms=%22whole%20 attitude%20was%20one%20of%20great%20calmness%20and%20courage%22.

77 "The Countess Who Became Heroine of the *Titanic*," Western Daily Press, January 30, 1998, https://www.newspapers.com/image/921936192/?match=1 &terms=%22Like%20an%20earthquake%20or%20a%20distant%20battle%22.

twenty-six thousand hours of rigorous manual labor on her birth; and in a mere three hours, she had been devoured by the elements.

There was something particularly ominous about the Atlantic's oceanic conditions the night *Titanic* sank. By all accounts, waters were unusually calm and flat as she floundered in panic. There was no passion to *Titanic*'s sinking as far as nature was concerned. The icy sea was as indifferent to the grandeur of the world's largest and fastest man-made moving object as it would have been to a ninety-foot schooner that sprung a leak. Somehow, *Titanic*'s sinking is even more traumatic and unjust in that nature did not even deem her a worthy opponent. Ships that sink in ferocious gales and violent breakers in stormy conditions are perhaps more logical in human cognition, but *Titanic* was forced to yield to apathetic nothingness. *Titanic* had no passionate warfare with another ship or the ocean's temperamental way; she sank in black, calm waters with no winds, choppy waves, or torrential ocean rains. As far as the North Atlantic Ocean was concerned, the forty-six-thousand-ton ship of dreams might as well have been a ship in a bottle.

ROWING

As Tom rowed with Noël's steering from the rear, the boat glided through flat ice and bodies of fellow passengers of all classes—those who had jumped or fallen from the rapid sinking of the once-opulent creature *Titanic*. Through yards of water and bodies, Lifeboat Number 8 rowed toward whatever the melding of the black sky and black waters held. Everything was black, and nature was dead-quiet as screams flew through the black in echoes encased by the steady music of Hartley's orchestra. After the screaming and melody stopped from distance and death, an even thicker quiet fell on those lifeboat survivors as the herd of them sailed on in a mosaic of grief, shock, and confusion. They took turns at the rows and tiller as sore muscles and the ice-cold air became too much. The countess recalled a faint light in the distance at one point while rowing:

> When the awful end came, I tried my best to keep the Spanish woman from hearing the agonizing sound of distress. They seemed to continue forever, although it could not have been more than ten minutes until the silence of a lonely sea dropped down. The indescribable loneliness, the ghastliness of our feelings never can be told. We tried to keep in touch with the other boats by shouting and succeeded fairly well. Our boat was the furthest away because we had chased the phantom lights for three hours. Yes, I rowed for three hours.[78]

> Oh, the pitiful sadness of our rowing, rowing toward the lights of a ship that disappeared ... We in boat No. 8 saw some tramp steamer's masthead lights, and then we saw the glow of red as she swung toward us for a few minutes. Then darkness and despair.[79]

The light lifeboats were straining toward was suddenly gone, and there were no visual points of reference in sight range to even row toward—just blackness pushing in. There was nothing to go

---

[78] "Horror of the Chase of the Phantom Light," *The Arkansas Gazette,* April 26, 1912, https://www.newspapers.com/image/138384366/?terms=%22whole%20attitude%20was%20one%20of%20great%20calmness%20and%20courage%22.

[79] "Vessel Near *Titanic?" The Washington Post,* April 22, 1912, https://www.newspapers.com/image/28898026/?match=1&terms=%22Miss%20Gladys%20Cherry%22.

back toward and nothing to go forward toward. The ship from which they disembarked was gone without so much as lingering ripples left on the surface. The ship toward which they were aiming was also gone, and eighteen to twenty little boats were left to float along Iceberg Alley with nothing between them and *Titanic*'s own fate but wooden slats. They rowed on at first in screams from a few passengers Noël quieted with compassion and then in utter silence.

New York Times bestselling author Elizabeth Kaye described the countess' lifeboat in her book *Lifeboat No. 8: An Untold Tale of Love, Loss, and Surviving the Titanic*:

> It was built to carry sixty-five passengers and measured 30 feet long, 9.1 feet wide, and 4 feet deep. It was a simple, sleek, and graceful structure that tapered to a point at the stern and at the bow and was fashioned from overlapping planks of white-painted yellow pine held by copper nails. The white interior had four wide seats made of pitch pine, as well as foot-wide planks for additional seating that ran the length of the boat on both sides. Beneath the seats were stowed three sets of heavy oars and a kerosene lamp.[80]

The few lamps the boats had seemed to be no match for the enveloping darkness of the ocean, but the scattered dots of gaslight were at least something. Though there were little if any visual stimuli to encourage survivors as they were moving toward safety, Gladys Cherry suggested auditory stimuli to lead them. She and Noël led those in Lifeboat Number 8 in song to collectively keep in hopeful spirits. One of the first to strengthen their resolve was, *Lead, Kindly*

---

80 Kaye, 257.

Light with the poignant refrain of "Lead Thou Me On," as night and unknown waters threatened on all sides, and the unsinkable ship of dreams was left to the sea's destruction. The countess rowed for five black hours. Tom Jones later recalled: "Sing, you say! I should think we did! It kept up our spirits. We sang as we rowed, all of us, starting out with 'Pull for the shore,' and we were still singing when we saw the lights of the *Carpathia*. Then we stopped singing, and prayed."[81]

CARDINAL SAINT JOHN HENRY NEWMAN

In June 1833, nearly eighty years before *Titanic* was even thought of, Cardinal Saint John Henry Newman wrote a poem called *Pillar of Cloud* that would prove to be a spiritual anchorage for the countess. While sailing the Mediterranean to Sicily, a thirty-two-year-old Newman became critically ill with what many now believe was scarlet fever. Never having particularly hearty health, he spent tortuous weeks recovering from his illness, where he underwent bloodletting sessions and eventually had to learn to walk and talk again. He said in a letter to a friend describing his wretched trip that he believed he would surely die, yet the Lord spared him. He interpreted this to mean that the Lord spared him for a specific purpose and his work was nowhere near complete.[82]

Newman was born in London on February 21, 1801, as the eldest of six to an upper-middle-class family. After graduating from Oxford's Trinity College at twenty, he earned a post-seminary fellowship

---

81 Tom Jones, "Countess of Rothes' Story: Her Ladyship in Charge of a Boat," *Gloucestershire Chronicle*, April 27, 1912, https://www.newspapers.com/image/793131796/?match=1&terms=%22Her%20Ladyship%20in%20Charge%20of%20a%20Boat%22.

82 John Henry Newman, *Apologia Pro Vita Sua: Being a Reply to a Pamphlet Entitled 'What, Then, Does Dr. Newman Mean?'* (London: Longman, Green, Longman, Roberts, and Green, 1864), 99.

and was eventually ordained as an Anglican priest in espousing the Calvinistic beliefs under which he was raised as a boy. In his priesthood, he brought reform through his writings of theology and philosophy, which challenged both Protestants and Roman Catholics. In 1845, he converted to Catholicism after years of intense spiritual exploration during which he wrote some of his most influential essays. He went on to establish Birmingham Oratory at Maryvale and later University College in Dublin. Newman died not long after Pope Leo XIII appointed him to the College of the Cardinals in 1879. Newman died on August 11, 1890, at the age of eighty-nine. In October 2019, he was canonized as a saint by the Catholic Church.

Upon his 1833 voyage back to England after battling his life and death illness, a weak, homesick Newman penned the poem *Pillar of Cloud* on the open seas. The poem was eventually published and put to music with the title changed to *Lead, Kindly, Light*. Newman recalled:

> Before starting from my inn, I sat down on my bed and began to sob bitterly. My servant, who had acted as my nurse, asked what ailed me. I could only answer, "I have a work to do in England." I was aching to get home, yet for want of a vessel I was kept at Palermo for three weeks. I began to visit the churches, and they calmed my impatience, though I did not attend any services. At last I got off in an orange boat, bound for Marseilles. We were becalmed for whole week in the Straits of Bonifacio, and it was there that I wrote the lines, *Lead, Kindly Light*, which have since become so well known.[83]

The inspiration for the work was drawn from the Book of Exodus's thirteenth chapter in which Moses leads the Israelites out of

---

[83] Ibid.

their Egyptian captivity at long last. The chapter describes a "pillar of cloud" that goes before them as they travel toward the Promised Land. *Lead, Kindly Light* was sung desperately from the lifeboats of *Titanic* in much the same way it had been written by Newman from within the slats of a boat with a similar longing for safe shore. He said of his initial trip to Italy, in hindsight, what remnants of *Titanic* surely felt of their own voyage from within the lifeboats, "And now will you say my expedition has been a failure? By no means. Do I repent of coming? Why, certainly I should not have come had I known that it was at the danger of my life."[84]

With nearly one hundred years between them, Newman and *Titanic* survivors shared the same spirit of languishing against current circumstances and longing for the guidance of God toward the figurative "Promised Land" of rescue as they sang:

> *Lead, kindly Light, amid th' encircling gloom,*
>
> *Lead Thou me on;*
>
> *The night is dark, and I am far from home,*
>
> *Lead Thou me on;*
>
> *Keep Thou my feet; I do not ask to see*
>
> *The distant scene; one step enough for me.*
>
> *I was not ever thus, nor prayed that Thou*
>
> *Shouldst lead me on;*
>
> *I loved to choose and see my path, but now*

---

84 John Henry Newman, "Letters and Correspondence 1833—Sicily: To F. Rogers, Esq.," *Newman Reader*, June 5, 1833, https://www.newmanreader.org/biography/mozley/volume1/file9.html.

84 LEAD THOU ME ON

> Lead Thou me on;
>
> I loved the garish day, and spite of fears,
>
> Pride ruled my will; remember not past years.
>
> So long Thy pow'r has blest me, sure it still
>
> Wilt lead me on,
>
> O'er moor and fen, o'er crag and torrent, till
>
> The night is gone,
>
> And with the morn those angel faces smile,
>
> Which I have loved long since, and lost awhile.[85]

Survivor reports suggest that *Lead, Kindly Light* had been sung in a religious service aboard *Titanic* before her iceberg collision, and Gladys' recommendation of it was heralded by the countess in encouraging fellow passengers away from destitution and onward toward rescue. Surely, Cardinal Saint Newman intended the hymn to be clung to in such times when night presses in with no glint of light just as it had served him on open seas of uncertainty after a tremendous fight for his life. The anthem that had carried him along the waves so carried more than seven hundred of *Titanic*'s survivors. Surely, the Lord led them all in the way of safe shore, going before them in Newman's referenced "pillar of cloud" over the black Atlantic waters.

---

85 Newman, *Lead, Kindly Light*.

CHAPTER FOUR
Carpathia

> *"The Countess of Rothes, who is an expert oarswoman, practically commanded her boat when she found the men could not row properly. Several women took the places of weak and unskilled stewards."*[86]

The countess rowed steadily with the dozens of others huddled in frozen grief around her. She and Tom took turns on positioning; but as badly as their muscles ached, nothing compared to the grief they carried. Everyone's emotions were paralyzed from the great loss of *Titanic* and hundreds of their fellow passengers but also from the fear of not being rescued quickly enough to delay their own deaths. Whatever emotional paralysis the countess may have endured never affected her physical resolve of forward motion toward their only hope.

Few lifeboats went back toward the wreckage site after *Titanic* had long since plummeted into the deep. The initial suction was a

---

86 "The Latest," *The Cobar Herald*, April 23, 1912, https://www.newspapers.com/image/969550216/?match=1&terms=%22she%20found%20the%20men%20could%20not%20row%22.

serious concern for lifeboat passengers, as well as the possibility of those in the water mobbing the boats, which could have resulted in even more chaos and death. The few lifeboats that did go back carefully dodged growlers, frozen bodies, and debris to retrieve the few handfuls of lone survivors who had miraculously survived both the final sinking and the frigid twenty-eight-degree Atlantic.

The countess, Cissy, and Gladys implored the others to allow their lifeboat to be among the ones to go back for other survivors floating among the debris. Tom Jones echoed their pleas; but the majority won out, and Lifeboat Number 8 did not go back. The screams of those they weren't permitted to save haunted them all, but especially Noël, for the rest of their lives.

The rowing was blistering hard in tandem with the frightful cold that enveloped the weary remnants of the world's unsinkable dream. For the countess, it wasn't at all like the rowing she enjoyed on pleasant boating trips she remembered from sunny bygone days in the earl's yacht in Fife. Her hands were numb from the freezing temperatures and splintered from the heavy wooden oars. Neither her ermine fur nor title made any difference in the black. To the Atlantic and her fellow passengers, she was just as much a rugged seaman as Tom carrying out Captain Smith's last orders of "Row straight for those ship lights over there." Just because the first light disappeared didn't mean his orders were negated. Surely, there would be another light if only that of dawn.

Clinging only to Hebrews 11:1 in their faith as "the substance of things hoped for, the evidence of things not seen," they rowed on. The air grew cooler in preparation of morning; and their refrains of hymns occasionally waned, prodded along only by the countess' natural fortitude through refrains of: "So long Thy pow'r has blest me, sure it still Wilt lead me on, O'er moor and fen, o'er crag and torrent, till The night is gone."[87]

Billows of despair, screams, and ice tears lingered long after the *Titanic* and her elegant orchestra sank. Surviving the sinking was only half the traumatic battle, for the more than seven hundred survivors threaded through the ice fields in lifeboats; surviving the cold, arduous wait to be rescued was quite another. Survivors were operating on very limited information compared to what we have in hindsight of the great disaster. We know how the story ends; but in the frightening oblivion between the safety of before and the safety of after—they were adrift in nothingness.

None were thinking, "If we can just row to the *Carpathia* we'll be fine." Survivors had limited information about surrounding ships and what, if any, notifications had been transmitted to or received by other ships or shore operators before *Titanic* went down. Surely, they asked themselves variations of: *What if no one knows of the sinking and we must plod along dying one by one? What if there are no other ships for hundreds of miles? What if shore is equally far? What if we, too, are abandoned to these same waters* Titanic *is? What if we survived the sinking only to meet a worse fate? How long must we row and toward what?*

As dawn finally began to break through the darkness of that horrible night, the smattering of cold, weary lifeboats saw another light they prayed wasn't the phantom from before. Weary survivors quickened with hope as they saw *RMS Carpathia* emerging from the icy sea mist. Everyone suddenly became

---

87 Newman, *Lead, Kindly Light*.

reenergized in their rowing and sat up a little straighter as rescue seemed imminent. Surely, this vessel would not pass them by as the other mystery ship had hours before. The closer to *Carpathia*'s hull, the more determined survivors' rowing and singing grew. Surely, God had led them through the darkest night any of them had ever experienced and toward this kindly light.

RESCUED BY CUNARD LINE

Everyone but perhaps J. Bruce Ismay was happy to see *Carpathia* steam toward them in preparing rescue efforts. Whatever disgrace *Titanic* had caused Ismay, having to rely on *Cunard* for assistance surely doubled.

Cunard's British liner *Carpathia* was launched in 1902 and named after the mighty European mountain range, the Carpathian Mountains, which form an arc that towers over Central Europe.[88] It was built by Swan and Hunter for *Cunard* not necessarily as a show ship like *Titanic*, but more of a sturdy passenger vessel of moderate capabilities. *Carpathia*'s Captain Arthur Henry Rostron had received Jack Phillips' distress calls when *Titanic* began its descent. And he had steamed off course to intercept survivors as quickly as possible, though at the time of transmission, *Carpathia* was some sixty miles away, making her at least four hours from *Titanic*'s last coordinates.

Carpathia had departed from New York City on April 11, 1912, with nearly 750 passengers traveling to Fiume (Rijeka, Croatia). Rostron led rescue efforts in pulling *Titanic* survivors from the

---

[88] Jack Beresford, "The Story of *RMS Carpathia*: 12 Incredible Facts About the Ship that Saved *Titanic*'s Survivors," *The Irish Post*, April 14, 2021, https://www.irishpost.com/life-style/rms-carpathia-12-facts-titanics-rescue-165987.

water to deliver them safely to their intended destination: New York Harbor.

Carpathia was a smaller, utilitarian ocean liner nearly 350 feet shorter in length than *Titanic* with a passenger capacity of seventeen hundred. The rather plain, dated ship steadied toward the boats with crewmen at the ready with rope ladders extending. By 8:30 a.m. on April 15, 1912, more than seven hundred *Titanic* survivors were drawn from the icy Atlantic and pulled aboard *Carpathia*. Lifeboat Number 2 arrived first with Lifeboat Number 8 close behind.

Throughout the dreadful hours of back-breaking rowing, Noël had been true to her commitment to Captain Smith's original orders, to her faith, and to the Leslie family motto of "grip fast." In fact, she had gripped the oars so tightly that her numbed hands had to be nearly pried from them as their tiny vessel sat before the hanging rope ladder extended from the side of *Carpathia*.

One by one, hundreds of witnesses to *Titanic*'s great launch and great destruction slowly and wearily filed up the rope ladder and on to safe, solid deck. Members of all three classes who had boarded *Titanic* with equal wonderment collapsed in relief among *Carpathia*'s stunned and curious passengers. Captain Rostron later said, "Devoutly thankful I was that the long race was over . . . but with that feeling was the veritable ache which the now certain knowledge of the liner's loss brought."[89] There were at least four who were found dead in lifeboats when pulled aboard *Carpathia*. Father Roger Anderson gave requiem mass.

---

89 Simon Medhurst, *Titanic: Day by Day* (Barnsley: Pen and Sword History, 2022), 129.

Frostbitten and weary beyond words, Noël had lost feeling in her hands hours before. They were too stiff to allow her to grip the rope ladder and pull her aboard. In her utter exhaustion, *Carpathia*'s crew extended a swing made of canvas and wood to lift her from Lifeboat Number 8. Many accounts say she fainted the moment her feet touched *Carpathia*'s deck.

ABOARD *CARPATHIA*

Carpathia was never officially requisitioned as a hospital ship; but to *Titanic* survivors, she was the world's best impromptu hospital ship. Crew and passengers alike tended to their newest passengers aboard with great compassion and quiet understanding. Many survivors suffered from varying extremes of hypothermia, dehydration, exhaustion, and utter shock, while some had died in the lifeboats unbeknownst to other passengers.

After resting and reviving with nourishment, Noël continued tending to those from her own lifeboat as well as other survivors huddling under wool blankets passed around from *Carpathia*'s crew. The "grip fast" motto was not just for the direst of hours, the countess believed. Though they had been saved, she continued in her commitment to serve her fellow survivors without regard for her royal name.

Though most were dazed from the wretched physical and emotional ordeal, J. Bruce Ismay must have carried great shame in having his marketplace nemesis rescue him along with hundreds of others who had put their utmost trust in *White Star Line*'s boasts of *Titanic*. Ismay was hoisted aboard in his pajamas.

Captain Rostron was eventually awarded a United States Congressional Gold Medal for his heroic efforts in tending to *Titanic* survivors, further staining *White Star Line*'s name. Captain Rostron was the first aboard *Carpathia* to give up his quarters as hospital triage. As commercial enemies, *Cunard* and *White Star* had scrimmaged over who had the most power and prestige on the high seas; but the proud *White Star Line* had to bow its head in great humility as *Carpathia* hoisted former *White Star* believers on deck. Ismay reportedly stayed holed up in his quarters for the entire voyage to New York, only allowing Captain Rostron to enter once briefly.

Titanic's sister *Olympic* initially offered to come pick up survivors from *Carpathia* so Rostron did not have to backtrack to New York; but everyone agreed that *Olympic* may have sent survivors into further hysterics if they were to see, out of the fog, a vision of *Titanic* sailing toward them to board as a mirror image of the ship they had just witnessed sink to the sea floor.

PASSENGERS ON CARPATHIA

Dozens of *Carpathia* passengers followed their captain's example and gave up their quarters so the newly aboard could have warm, comfortable accommodations. Many of *Carpathia*'s men gladly slept in deck chairs or makeshift cots on open deck so women and children could have their beds in which to begin their layered recoveries. These selfless acts served as further dismantling of the longstanding traditional class system.

Noël, like Ismay, was given one of the finest staterooms aboard *Carpathia*, which would have barely been considered a second-class suite aboard *Titanic*. One of the first things Noël did after coming around from her fatigue-faint was to send a message to Norman and her parents ashore letting them know she survived.[90]

Captain Rostron closely monitored outgoing messages and refused to transmit many for fear that releasing too much information too soon about the disaster might make trouble ashore before any official inquiry. After Noël notified her family of her general safe status, she got back to work not on her own recovery but that of others of all classes.[91]

It would have been easy enough for Noël to stay holed up in her quarters and succumb to the fatigue she carried, and no one could have blamed her. Instead, she used her Red Cross nursing skills learned under their Scotland initiative to tend to those aboard. There weren't many women of nobility who possessed the skills needed for emergency medicine. Noël could have pulled rank at any time and chose instead to rest privately rather than bustle about tending to the needs of others, but she didn't. She cared for her fellow survivors with soup, blankets, tranquilizers, and bandages, with no regard for class just as fervently as she had tilled the lifeboat. She was a florid portrait of the gospel for those who so desperately needed reminding of hope after such a black, desperate night.

The countess' cousin, Gladys, also joined her in tending efforts: "Our *Titanic* men, with legs and feet frozen, are wonderful when you think of what they have been through . . . a cheery face and

---

[90] George Behe, *Voices from the Carpathia: Rescuing RMS Titanic* (Gloucestershire: The History Press, 2015), 72.
[91] Daniel Allen Butler, *The Other Side of the Night: The Carpathia, The Californian, and the Night Titanic Was Lost* (Havertown, PA: Casemate, 2009), 2248.

word did so much for them . . . Noël and I have helped in seeing after these poor distressed souls, and it has helped us so much."[92]

Though the countess would never have publicly told of doing so, other passengers recalled the impromptu sewing circle she organized on deck to fit second and third-class children, many of whom were French or Irish immigrants, with dry, warm clothes. Many had been pulled aboard *Carpathia* in ragged pajamas, threads for coats, and wet stockings—if any at all. Noël used the ship's extra supply of plain woolen blankets to cut and sew into fine garments custom-made by a countess.[93]

One of the saddest stories of *Titanic* was that of Rhoda Abbott. Noël's heart ached for Rhoda as she came to know her story in *Carpathia*'s steerage. Rhoda was the only female to be pulled from the waters when lifeboats went back to collect anyone in the waves still alive. Rhoda was born in Buckinghamshire in 1873, making her just a handful of years older than Noël. She had been married to professional boxer, Stanton Abbott, but divorced him barely a year before she and their two sons, Rossmore, sixteen, and Eugene, thirteen, boarded *Titanic*. As a single, working mother, Rhoda believed her family's future to be bright in moving to America, so she and her sons secured third-class tickets on *Titanic*.[94]

The Abbotts were lucky enough to be ushered to top deck just before *Titanic* sank. Rhoda was offered a seat in the last remaining lifeboat but did not take it because her sons were told they could not join her. She gave up her seat in the lifeboat and tightly held

---

92 Bigham, *A Matter of Course*.
93 Medhurst, *Titanic: Day by Day*, 360.
94 Robert L. Bracken, "The Mystery of Rhoda Abbott Revealed," *Encyclopedia-Titanica*, last modified June 7, 2004, https://www.encyclopedia-titanica.org/rhoda-abbott.html.

Rossmore and Eugene until the terrible end when the last of the ship sank. All three were swept from the deck and each other's clutches, and Rhoda never saw her sons alive again. She swam to Collapsible Boat A, which had also been swept off the deck. Though dozens more around her died, Rhoda eventually boarded one of the lifeboats that reversed toward the wreckage.

She suffered, like hundreds of others, from hypothermia. So severe was the damage to her legs that she could not walk for days after rescue. She was hospitalized in New York's St. Vincent's Hospital after *Carpathia* docked and remained in doctors' care for weeks. Rhoda's story deeply moved Noël as it was relayed in fragments while she tended to the wounded woman. Noël paid for Rhoda's hospital stay and gave her funds to reestablish herself in the United States.[95]

Noël embodied Christ's work of bowing her royal rank in tenderness to the wants and needs of society's definition of "lowliest." The countess was, for many, a paragon of redemption after so much had been lost the evening before. While she never preached or prodded, her kind, careful acts of service aboard both Lifeboat Number 8 and *Carpathia* were the much-needed anecdote after such destruction and death. She quickly became known among her fellow passengers as "the plucky little countess" for her bravery and impartial compassion.

The crew of the *RMS Carpathia* noted the countess' curious servitude of her fellow survivors. An attendant on the ship working alongside Noël in tending to survivors eventually realized what nobility she was in the midst of. When she discovered this

---

[95] Bracken, "The Mystery of Rhoda Abbott Revealed."

woman who so tirelessly dressed wounds, rocked crying children, and fetched blankets and bowls of soup by the dozens was, in fact, the Countess of Rothes, she said, "You have made yourself famous by rowing in the boat."

Noël replied, "I hope not. I have done nothing."[96]

Noël was one of the more than seven hundred to survive the *Titanic* but the only countess to steer a lifeboat and its passengers to safety. Her anthem rang in the ears of many for days after:

> *Lead, kindly light, amid the encircling gloom*
>
> *Lead thou me on!*
>
> *The night is dark, and I'm far from home*
>
> *Lead thou me on!*[97]

As "scandalous" as it may have been under normal circumstances, Tom and Noël met again aboard *Carpathia* after having served so peculiarly together. Few were going by rules even hours after the tragedy that so unraveled the rigid social mores of the era. The two spoke with their kindred spirits more than their words, and they exchanged addresses to keep in touch—not that they would ever forget each other, but it seemed important to them both to still "hold on," even though imminent danger had passed. They each held great respect and sincere love for one another for the rest of their lives because of their desperate, unlikely meeting aboard Lifeboat Number 8.

---

96 Kaye, 613.
97 Newman, *Lead, Kindly Light*.

RECOVERY EFFORTS

As survivors steamed toward New York on *Carpathia*, the Halifax cable ship *Mackay-Bennett* embarked for *Titanic*'s last known coordinates off the coast of Newfoundland to recover what bodies she left behind. There were other ships accompanying *Mackay-Bennett* in their *White Star Line* contracted expedition to retrieve the dead, but *Mackay-Bennett* would go down in history as *Titanic*'s coffin ship.

Generally, captains and crew hired in the effort knew they might need to transport batches of bodies to shore, but nothing could have prepared them for the scene they came upon in Iceberg Alley. Equipped with cutters and coffins, dozens of crewmen, from the seasick novice to the most experienced seaman, spent nearly two weeks at sea for the sake of *Titanic*'s dead.

With a few over seven hundred survivors aboard *Carpathia*, *White Star Line* had prepared crews that more than fifteen hundred bodies were unaccounted for. The promise of double wages was little consolation for the grisly duty required of crews. The aftermath of the wreckage site was something that would haunt those men for the rest of their lives. Their view surely wasn't unlike that of Captain Wilhelm of the German liner *Bremen*, who passed over *Titanic*'s wreckage site just before the bodies were recovered. *The San Francisco Call and Post* reported, "Women fainted in hysterics at the horror scene, and tonight Captain Wilhelm was scarcely able to speak of his experience. 'I have been to sea for 23 years,' said the captain, 'but never have I looked upon a sight like that—a livid sea of human bodies.' Wilhelm said he counted 125 bodies and then stopped."[98]

---

[98] "Bremen Plowed Through Bodies," *The San Francisco Call and Post*, April 25, 1912, https://www.newspapers.com/image/80851571/?match=1&terms=%22Women%20fainted%20in%20hysterics%20at%20the%20horror%20scene%22.

Crews needed no compass to know exactly where *Titanic* went down. The floating bunches of bodies and debris were the only markers crews needed. Water-logged remnants of tables, doors, an overturned lifeboat, a drowning book here, and a stray lifebelt bobbing there dotted the seascape for yards and yards.

The eerily calm sea of glass from the night *Titanic* sank was long gone with the ship. It was a choppy, angry sea that recovery teams had to contend with, making it an arduous process to pull frozen, water-bloated bodies from the waves. Crews encountered mangled remains of those injured by the sinking and those with calm almost pleasant expressions frozen across their faces. Frozen women were found clutching frozen children, glassy-eyed with terror etched as their eternal countenance.

The crew hoisted men, women, babies, and dogs from the waters with poles; documented what they could; and once again divided into classes. Assumptions about appearance, clothing, and identifiable accessories were used as determining metrics when true identification was unavailable. It is unfathomable to think the jewelry or garment a victim was found in became the voice that decided their funeral, but the class system often persisted in death for those of the era. Persons perceived as members of first class, perhaps from jewels around their necks or soaked remains of their first-class ticket found in their pockets, were prepared for embalming and land burial. Even in their class divisions, many bodies remained nameless with only scant hints of their identities.[99]

---

99   Ibid.

There were only so many coffins and so much weight these recovery vessels could carry; so many crew members and second and third-class passengers were wrapped in canvas, stacked, and tied with weights to join their fellow passengers in the black depths of the ocean. Rev. C.K. Hinds was aboard *Mackay-Bennett* to bless those buried beneath the waves in a mass funeral. The reverend later said of his appointment, "Anyone attending a burial at sea will most surely lose the common impression of the awfulness of a grave in the mighty deep. The wild Atlantic may rage and toss but far below in the calm untroubled depth they rest in peace."[100]

Crews recovered more than two hundred bodies from the ravages of the North Atlantic. About 150 victims were taken to Halifax for burial, while more than one hundred others were weighted down and buried at sea. Those towed to Halifax were either claimed by family and buried in their own communities or buried in Halifax's Fairview Lawn, Mount Olivet, or Baron de Hirsch. John Jacob Astor IV's son offered crews thousands of dollars for the recovery of his father's body, and his was among those first-class passengers' retrieved. He was buried in Manhattan.

Grown men cried, vomited, and fell silent as they did the work few possessed the courage to do. Many of them felt as though *White Star Line* executives themselves should have had to send these poor souls to their final resting place in their stead for all the smoking room boasting they had done ashore.

Weather conditions of cold rain and fog caused *Carpathia* to creep back toward New York's harbor, compared to her usual

---

100 "Service Over Each of the 116 Bodies Buried at Sea," *St. Louis Post Dispatch*, May 1, 1912, https://www.newspapers.com/image/138924026/?match=1&terms=%22Mackay-Bennett%22.

average of fifteen knots. After three days of slow and steady traveling, the *Carpathia* arrived in New York with more than fourteen hundred passengers on April 18, 1912. This was not the way any of *Titanic*'s survivors had envisioned arriving in New York when they boarded *White Star*'s ship of dreams just eight days before.

IN NEW YORK

The world outside of *Titanic*'s survivors knew nothing of the unique suffering endured in the irreconcilable contrast of grandeur and downfall. For the rest of their lives, survivors of all classes carried with them a deep-seated helplessness from witnessing thousands at their fingertips slowly meet their death without even a chance at deliverance. The unstoppable destruction survivors witnessed far surpassed their cases of frostbite and fatigue, and explaining to the world ashore what and how their beloved ship of dreams died was another feat all its own.

The world had held its collective breath for *Titanic*'s maiden voyage, as many around the globe had known of her since her birth in Belfast's shipyard and the promise of power and prestige she represented. To tell them that their idea of *Titanic* was all a terrible mirage and the unsinkable was lying mangled and defeated at the bottom of the ocean was something that would take years to fully communicate and perhaps all of eternity to understand.

With only the wireless to bridge the gap between water and land, the first hint of disaster only came ashore in ripples. Initially, the world only knew of technological trouble with *Titanic*'s Marconi's wireless invention. Newspapers reported that other ships and shore had lost wireless connection with *Titanic*, which certainly caused concern but not panic.

Just a few hours after *Titanic* sank, the United Press's delayed report flew around the globe that though *White Star Line* had temporarily lost communication with the vessel unexpectedly, there was surely no danger. *White Star Line*'s executive, Philip "P.A." Franklin assured the world through United Press correspondents that *Titanic* was "in no danger: satisfied liner is unsinkable!"[101] Franklin was quoted many times in variations of reassurance that "while we are not in direct communication with the *Titanic*, we are perfectly satisfied that the ship cannot be sunk."[102]

Through ships that received *Titanic*'s distress calls, news of the collision came ashore shortly after reports that communication had been lost. Franklin again rushed to reassure the masses that the darling of the *White Star Line* was impervious to danger as detailed in Washington D.C.'s *Evening Star*:

> We place absolute confidence in the *Titanic*. We believe the boat is absolutely unsinkable and although she may have sunk at the head of the bow, we know the boat would remain on the water. We do not attach any significance to the fact that there are no Marconi messages being received from the boat. We think it denotes nothing but the fact that the boat is in communication with other steamers, for she may have gotten off all the messages she wanted to send.[103]

---

101 Philip Albright Franklin, "Says Vessel is Unsinkable," *The Evening Star*, April 15, 1912, https://www.newspapers.com/image/331610978/?match=1&terms=%22We%20place%20absolute%20confidence%20in%20the%20Titanic%22.
102 Ibid.
103 Philip Albright Franklin, "Passengers of *Titanic* in Crash with Iceberg, Safe on Other Vessels," Evening Star, April 15, 1912, https://www.newspapers.com/image/331611150/?match=1&terms=%22gotten%20off%20all%20the%20messages%20she%20wanted%20to%20send%22.

Franklin may be the poster child for how not to provide official statements for corporate public relations, as he would soon regret his sugary bravado. Because of the delay in communicating through wireless, it is hard to know if Franklin's statements were intentionally deceiving or simply further exhibitions of *White Star*'s arrogant denial; but either way, days after the disaster, millions were led to believe that *Titanic* and her passengers were perfectly safe, just temporarily unavailable through wireless.

There were numerous erroneous reports circulated by a combination of too-anxious reporters, misinformation, and speculation. For example, all of London went to bed on April 17 believing that though *Titanic* had collided with an iceberg, all of her passengers had been saved and the ship herself was being towed to port, while the *New York American* reported the same day that eighteen hundred lives were lost in the sinking.

Even as *Carpathia* made her way to New York with traumatized survivors, the world was being subjected to more of White Star Line's narrow rhetoric: "We are absolutely satisfied that even if she was in collision with an iceberg, she is in no danger," Franklin said.[104] White Star Line would once again regret their boasting as the world began to learn the true fate of their gloried *Titanic*.

PIER 59

It was a cold, rainy night on April 18. The *Carpathia* steamed through the Hudson River and passed her own dock number of fifty-four. Much to the confusion of many onlookers, *Carpathia*

---

104 Philip Albright Franklin, "Absolutely Unsinkable," *Binghamton Press and Leader*, April 15, 1912, https://www.newspapers.com/image/252511742/?match=1&terms=%22Franklin%22%20and%20%22Titanic%22.

entered *Titanic*'s dock number fifty-nine. They docked long enough to drop off *Titanic*'s empty lifeboats. Many reports say there were over one hundred thousand people who had swarmed New York's docks to witness confirmation of the rumors that, despite *White Star Line*'s claims, *Titanic* had, in fact, sunk, leaving hundreds to be carried ashore by *Carpathia*. Dusts of lanterns and flashbulbs were the only light by which to see in the faces of survivors that *White Star Line*'s claims—from the beginning—carried with them only devastation. From Pier 59 back to fifty-four, *Carpathia* had been escorted by the *USS Chester*, a small scout cruiser, with the solemnity of a watery funeral procession. At *Cunard*'s given Pier 54, finally, passengers had reached safe port. *Carpathia*'s original passengers went gallantly ahead of *Titanic*'s survivors down the gangway to prevent mass hysteria when survivors first appeared. No one spoke, for there was nothing to say. The Earl of Rothes waited with bated breath on the pier for the first glimpse of his Noël.

Captain Rostron thought perhaps having his passengers go first, the blend of passengers of all classes from *Titanic* disembarking afterward wouldn't be as obvious and startling to the crowds below. He was wrong. Many survivors, regardless of class, still wore patchwork coverings from their fight for survival; and their disheveled state was something a few bowls of soup and warm blankets couldn't conceal.

The rain knocked down on the throngs of people and black umbrellas in a cadence of grief. Some said the rain that night wasn't rain at all but Heaven's tears for the death of thousands of people, the *Titanic* herself, and the Edwardian dream of it all. In looking into the grief-stricken faces of survivors, thousands came to admit that man could not build something from the merger of Heaven and earth, Mount Olympus was just a myth, and no ship is unsinkable.

IN THE AFTERMATH

Officers stood by to escort survivors to refuge. The more than seven hundred were dispersed throughout New York hospitals and hotels, including Hotel Chelsea for first- and second-class passengers just a few steps away from where *Carpathia* docked, and The Jane Hotel for third-class passengers and crew. The earl swept the countess from the pier, and both held on too tightly. She later said to *The Los Angeles Daily Times*, "I was glad beyond expression to see my husband waiting to receive me as I stepped from the steamer. I hope that I, nor anyone else, will ever have to undergo another such catastrophe. I thank God I was saved and I only wish all of the poor souls who perished might have had similar good fortune."[105]

Norman had secured accommodations at the Ritz-Carlton Hotel for himself, Noël, and Cissy. He had the room overwhelmed with spring flowers and engaged attending physician, Dr. Edward Dinkelapiel, for Noël and Cissy both. As *The Daily Telegraph* reported back to her beloved England on her condition, "It is not so much exposure and shock which have made her ill, as the effects of her hard labor in pulling at

---

[105] "Countess of Rothes Here After *Titanic* Experience," The Los Angeles Daily Times, May 16, 1912, https://www.newspapers.com/image/380257771/?terms=%22I%20was%20glad%20beyond%20expression%20to%20see%20my%20husband%22.

the oars. Her boat was likewise undermanned because the crew preferred to stay behind."[106]

As honorable and selfless as it was for the countess to step down from peerage when disaster arose and pull more than her weight in rescue efforts, some of the older British elite found her heroism to be a gaudy display. What woman of noble title would hike up her satin evening gown and row a lifeboat like a common seaman? For all the Victorian etiquette, waltzes, and traditional cotillions in which she was proficient, the skills that saved her life and the lives of many others were the gritty, laborious ones of rowing and nursing.

Survivors wilted into their respective New York accommodations, trying desperately to find illusive composure on the other side of warm rest. The crowds on the waterfront were hungry for details and explanations to bridge the gap between *White Star*'s delusionary story and the grim reality they saw in the faces of survivors. It became quickly apparent to the world that not only was *Titanic* utterly sinkable, like any other mortal-made ship, but also that in her falter, she had taken more than fifteen hundred lives with her.

The day after *Carpathia*'s New York arrival was the earl and countess' twelfth wedding anniversary, and it passed strangely with promises of future celebrations under happier conditions. The same day, the United States Senate held a hearing about the maritime disaster at what was then the luxury hotel Waldorf-Astoria in Midtown Manhattan, built by American businessman,

---

106 "Heroic Conduct of Women Survivors," *The Daily Telegraph*, April 22, 1912, https://www.newspapers.com/image/818665953/?terms=%22Her%20boat%20was%20likewise%20undermanned%22.

John Jacob Astor IV, who lost his life on *Titanic*. At the time of his death, Astor was considered one of the wealthiest men in the world, furthering the existential truth that even great wealth and class distinction couldn't have prevented what only humility could have.

MEMORIAL

When survivors awoke in their New York quarters after the first land rest they had had in two weeks, newspapers reported scads of memorial services across the globe for those who perished aboard *Titanic*. England observed *Titanic*'s loss in a national day of mourning. More than five thousand people gathered at St. Paul's Cathedral in London to memorialize the ship and those who perished along with her. In Queenstown, officials flew flags at half-staff to honor the people of Ireland who went down with the ship of dreams.[107]

Protestant and Roman Catholic churches around the world converted their usual weekend religious services into memorial services for *Titanic*'s dead. The requiem held at New York's Madison Avenue Reformed Church of the Incarnation was attended by several survivors, where Rev. Dr. William Carter chose Psalm 93:3-4 as the crux of his sermon: "The floods have lifted up their voice; the floods lift up their waves. The LORD on high is mightier than the noise of many waters, yea, than the mighty waves of the sea."[108]

---

[107] "London Incidents: Memorial Service at St. Paul's Cathedral," *The Western Times*, April 20, 1912, https://www.newspapers.com/image/816846818/?match=1&terms=%22London%20Incidents%22.

[108] William Carter, "Requiem for *Titanic*'s Dead," *The Rutland Herald*, April 22, 1912, https://www.newspapers.com/image/533741328/?match=1&terms=%22The%20floods%20have%20lifted%22.

Dr. Carter also went on to rebuke boastful self-reliance, such as *White Star Line*'s: "The irony of it all was that the very bulk of the *Titanic*, which the builders said could weather any gale, withstand any shock, and was absolutely unsinkable, was the very thing that sent her more quickly to her doom."[109] Newspapers became the ongoing memorial of *Titanic*, with lengthy emotional tributes tucked in every edition for months after. Reports of eyewitness testimony and official inquiry particulars had newspapers ripped from the hands of street sellers across the world; for everyone, in nearly every country, had some claim, some connection to the ship they had followed since her birth and wanted to drink in all the fragments of explanation they could. *The Buffalo News* reported, "Representatives of nearly every foreign government called at the British Foreign Office yesterday [April 19, 1912] to express sympathy, and what money can do to alleviate the sufferings will readily be done. All appeals are meeting with generous response."[110]

Titanic boasted of British, Irish, and American nationalism. But she had been the world's ship; and in her death, the world mourned.

INQUIRY

On the other side of the bone-trembling fear, some survivors grew angry in their recovery. Many first-class widows—such as Mrs. Renee Harris, who lost her husband, millionaire Broadway producer, Henry B. Harris—loudly condemned *White Star Line*

---

109 Ibid.
110 "English Press Pays Tribute to Heroes," *The Buffalo News*, April 20, 1912, https://www.newspapers.com/image/352613324/?match=1&terms=%22All%20appeals%20are%20meeting%20with%20generous%20response%22.

from the safety of shore. Renee deemed her husband's death a murder at the hands of *White Star Line* officials:

> Fifteen hundred people were not drowned on the *Titanic*; fifteen hundred people were murdered, cruelly and foully murdered—that's the story, the true story of this awful wreck, I shall tell the world the second I am able . . . I was the last woman to leave the deck of that ship. I was put into a collapsible boat along with two other women and scores of the crew, women and children—and our husbands—were torn from us so the men of the crew could go along. But I am glad I waited. I had a few extra minutes with my husband—and I learned why the boat went to her grave—I learned of the carelessness with which she was handled, which amount to murder—plain, cold blooded murder.[111]

The US Senate conducted an eighteen-day investigation into hoards of claims similar to Renee's led by Michigan Senator William Alden Smith. Proceedings began in New York, moved to Washington D.C.'s Russell Senate Office Building for a time, and concluded on May 25, 1912, upon return to New York. The US investigation overlapped with the inquiry made by the British Wreck Commissioner for the British Board of Trade. Their inquiry lasted from May 2 to July 3 under John Charles Bigham, 1st Viscount Mersey, "Lord Mersey." Such inquiries were rooted in marine safety issues so *Titanic* wouldn't be a repeat event, but

---

[111] "Asleep in the Cradle of the Deep While Civilized World is Mourning," *The Daily Gate City*, April 21, 1912, https://www.newspapers.com/image/328430903/?match=1&terms=%22Asleep%20in%20the%20Cradle%20of%20the%20Deep%22.

the sensationalism of the ship and her mysterious ending added intrigue to collecting survivor accounts.

J. Bruce Ismay was subpoenaed along with surviving officers and crew to give testimony as to what could have possibly gone wrong to cause such carnage. Captains and crew members from other ships, maritime experts, and survivors of all classes were called in to piece together the reality that was so contrary to *White Star Line*'s promises in *Titanic*'s development.

Tom Jones was also called in for inquiry where he gave the following testimony of Noël:

> Senator Newlands. Can you give me the names of any passengers on your boat?
>
> Mr. Jones. One lady. She had a lot to say, and I put her to steering my boat.
>
> Senator Newlands. What was her name?
>
> Mr. Jones. Lady Rothe. She was a Countess or something.[112]

Noël managed to avoid cross-examination during both the US and British official inquiries, though she did send in an affidavit with her testimony during the British inquiry. After Lord Mersey made the blanket assumption that "all women" in Lifeboat Number 8 refused to return to the wreckage for survivors in the water, Noël indignantly set the record straight in her affidavit.

---

[112] "United States Senate Inquiry, Day 7," *Titanic Inquiry Project*, accessed January 20, 2024, https://www.titanicinquiry.org/USInq/AmInq07Jones01.php.

She clarified that she, Gladys Cherry, Cissy, an American lady aboard, and Tom all pleaded with the others to go back; yet they had been overruled by the hysterical majority in the boat, making it unsafe for everyone to go against them. Lord Mersey modified his statement based on Noël's passionate rebuttal and changed his "all women" to "some women" in Lifeboat Number 8.

As most inquiries are, *Titanic*'s were long, tedious, and messy with overlaps, biases, contradictions, and unanswerable questions. On May 28, 1912, the 1,145-page summary of the inquiry was presented to the United States Senate. The inquiries found that there was gross negligence on the part of *Titanic*'s officers in being unprepared for and indifferent to the need for an emergency evacuation. Captain Smith was accused of recklessness in *Titanic*'s speed, his refusal to heed icefield warnings, and his overall unprofessional response to the collision and evacuation procedures that caused great loss of life.

Captain James H. Moore of the *Mount Temple*, which was among the ships that also received the same icefield warnings over the wireless that *Titanic* had the night she sank, was quick to denounce Captain Smith's judgment. He called him "most unwise" to rush through Iceberg Alley at twenty-two-and-a-half knots in a blatant refusal to heed multiple warnings.[113]

Both US and British inquiry findings would forever stain Captain Edward John Smith's legacy, though he had, in the end, stood with tradition and went down with his ship. In her great empathy, the countess refused to join popular opinion and

---

113 "*Titanic* Hearing," *Boston Evening Transcript*, April 27, 1912, https://www.newspapers.com/image/735684965/?match=1&terms=%22most%20unwise%22.

forever lauded Captain Smith a calm and courageous leader under the most impossible circumstances.

Newspaper reporters were eager to conduct their own inquiries one witness at a time. The Countess of Rothes was one of the gracious few who, after much badgering, agreed to sit for an exclusive interview with *The New York Herald* on April 22, 1912.

CHAPTER FIVE
The End of an Era

"The Countess of Rothes, meeting the terrible ordeal so courageously, keeping her wits so thoroughly that she was chosen by the rough men with her in a drifting boat as their commander, is an example all womankind may well hold up to admiration."[114]

Norman, Noël, and Cissy remained at the Ritz-Carlton for several days to regain their bearings. After much rest, Noël organized a group with other first-class women who were also a bit stranded in New York without their wardrobes. The women went on a shopping spree like they never had before. Though bittersweet, it was empowering for the group to jointly replenish their empty closets with all New York's finest department stores had to offer. Naturally, one of their first stops was their lost fellow *Titanic* passenger Isidor Strauss' legendary Macy's at Herald Square.

Though *Titanic* cost approximately $7.5 million to construct, she was only collectively insured for $5 million for her hull and

---

114 "The Women of the *Titanic*," *The New York Times*, April 21, 1912, https://www.newspapers.com/image/26042879/?match=1&terms=%22meeting%20the%20terrible%20ordeal%20so%20courageously%22.

mechanics. Many survivors and victim estates filed claims for more than $12 million, citing expensive lost possessions, lost loved ones, and punitive damages for pain and suffering.

Noël filed a claim for more than $10,000 for the loss of her personal property left aboard the liner. She detailed the loss of a diamond marquis ring; centuries-old Brussels lace that had adorned her satin gown as a new bride when she had been presented at Buckingham Palace; and sets of black fox, seal, and ermine fur coats, along with her up-to-the-minute chic wardrobe she never traveled without. Claims of other survivors surpassed $50,000.[115]

Noël's exclusive interview with *The New York Herald* was syndicated around the world with additions, subtractions, and errors that rippled in stories and sub-stories. *The Washington Post* first printed the edited version of her interview with variations following:

> The earl of Rothes' family, on being interviewed, said that the Countess of Rothes could not be called an athlete or a sportswoman in any sense of the word. To describe her as an expert oarswoman was "wrong." Nevertheless the Countess of Rothes seems to have done sterling work and to have been comfort and inspiration to other women. Perhaps she recalled the family motto, "Grip fast!"[116]

With the interviewer, she solemnly concluded her account by saying, with cracked voice, "Brave men all that stood back so

---

115 "Echoes of Great Disaster," *The Kingston Daily Standard*, October 21, 1913, https://www.newspapers.com/image/785903039/?match=1&terms=%22Titanic%22.

116 "Snapshots at Social Leaders," *The Washington Post*, April 25, 1912, https://www.newspapers.com/image/28899455/?match=1&terms=%22Perhaps%20she%20recalled%20the%20family%20motto%22.

that women should have at least a chance to live. Their memory should be held sacred in the mind of the world forever."[117]

MOVING ON

After several more days of rest in New York after giving the interview to *The New York Herald*, the earl and countess went on to Pasadena, California, where they were to originally celebrate their wedding anniversary. It had been twelve years since Norman and Noël vowed themselves to one another before God and loved ones in St. Mary Abbots. The Rothes' celebration that *Titanic* had postponed required particularly special fittings as Norman praised the heavens *Titanic* had not made him a widower.

The couple lounged gaily in the private orchard cottage framed by thick orange trees. The sunshine and sweet perfume of the grove seemed to cling to their cottage walls and lighten the burden April 15 had caused. Ultimately, the Rothes decided against purchasing the orange grove Norman had been eyeing as an investment, but the respite the two enjoyed in balmy Southern California was priceless in their joint recovery. The countess told *The Los Angeles Daily Times*, "I am so glad to get to beautiful California where I can rest in the sunshine and among the flowers after my trying experience. All this is so pleasant after what we encountered on the cold seas floating among the cakes of ice."[118]

---

[117] "Horror of the Chase of the Phantom Light," *The Arkansas Gazette*, April 26, 1912, https://www.newspapers.com/image/138384366/?terms=%22whole%20attitude%20was%20one%20of%20great%20calmness%20and%20courage%22.

[118] "Countess of Rothes Here After *Titanic* Experience," *The Los Angeles Daily Times*, May 16, 1912, https://www.newspapers.com/image/380257771/?terms=%22I%20was%20glad%20beyond%20expression%20to%20see%20my%20husband%22.

LEAD THOU ME ON

Norman and Noël returned home to Leslie House in May of 1912, where the couple was greeted by seas of flag-waving, teary-eyed Scottish tenants who had anxiously read of her ordeal in passage to America. The Women's Unionist Association that Noël was chairwoman of hosted an elaborate celebration at Leslie House for her safe return and exercise in valor.

Thomas, Clementina, and their Southwest England community were quick to publicly thank God for keeping Noël safe in their statements printed by *The Gloucester Journal* in gathering for The English Church Union:

> Gloucester desires to proffer its deep sympathy with its late chairman (Mr. T. Dyer Edwardes) in the terrible anxiety he and Mrs. Dyer Edwardes have experienced by the deplorable accident to the *Titanic*, and to express its deep thankfulness to Almighty God for having preserved their daughter, the Countess of Rothes, in such deadly peril, as well as to offer the Countess sincere felicitations on her miraculous escape and conspicuous bravery.[119]

CATALYST

In his book *The Ship of Dreams: The Sinking of the Titanic and the End of the Edwardian Era*, Gareth Russel quotes a maritime historian who said *Titanic*'s sinking was "so shattering, so demoralizing that it was looked upon as the beginning of the end of the British Empire." Russell argues that:

---

[119] "The English Church Union: Meeting in Gloucester," *The Gloucester Journal*, May 4, 1912, https://www.newspapers.com/image/792539756/?match=1&terms=%22Gloucester%20desires%20to%20proffer%20its%20deep%20sympathy%20with%20its%20late%20chairman%22

> Truthfully, the *Titanic* disaster had no real political impact, beyond perhaps mildly exacerbating resentment in certain left-wing circles against the wealthy. The story that the steerage passengers were deliberately prevented from having a fair chance at escape fueled, but did not create, a conspiracy-heavy view of social relations on the eve of the First World War. In 1912, the recently formed British Seafarers' trade union had seen in the *Titanic* proof that "the ruling class rob and plunder the people all the time, and the Inquiry has shown that they have no scruples in taking advantage of death and disaster. Who needs sharks?"[120]

The truth lies, perhaps, somewhere in between the opposing views of this quoted maritime historian and Russell. There may not have been the kind of immediate, obvious sociopolitical change that often comes with the death of a ruler or initiation of a war, but there was a certain mix of Victorian and Edwardian ideology that did begin to die with the *Titanic* as a result of her sinking.

The humanity of the thing was difficult to look at through the class designations, and all kinds of people broke the rules along the route to survival or attempts at survival. Noël Leslie, Countess of Rothes, was one of the most noted figures who broke gender, class, and nobility "rules" to follow the light and lead others to it. Those accounts weren't easy for the world to sweep under the rug of division. *Titanic* didn't change the world overnight, but it was a catalyst in the breakdown of class system toxicity and its societal implications. *Titanic*'s captivating story poses tough questions that challenge everyone's sense of the

---

120 Russell, 321.

comfortable and predictable. The official inquiries brought up universal topics of trust, accountability, sound judgment, and preparedness—and the world had its ear to the door. The inquiries and reports of such also spotlighted the hypocrisy of "power and prestige" ideals in relation to Christian disciplines.

Certainly, the narrative of *Titanic* that emerged from the wreckage and those that helped shape it in their newspaper reports maintained the rhetoric of the era, but that spotlights the hypocrisy all the more. For example, despite there being more third-class passengers aboard *Titanic* than first- and second-class put together, many newspapers just after the disaster reported that most passengers on *Titanic* were of First and Second Class. The mourning the world did, however, did not take class distinction into account, and that was a start.

Among the most practical changes that emerged from the disaster related to maritime safety. After *Titanic*'s loss, *Olympic* was pulled from the waters for safety modifications. In 1913, the International Ice Patrol was created by the US Coast Guard to warn against icebergs in the Atlantic.

In reality, all the rigidity surrounding the issue of the class system and maintaining serious distinction between first, second, and third class came to nothing in the context of *Titanic*. Baptist minister Vance Havner summed up the fallout of that historically accepted discrimination after *Titanic*:

> I remember when the *Titanic* sank in 1912, it was the ship that was supposed to be unsinkable. The only thing it ever did was sink. When it took off from England, all kinds of passengers were aboard—millionaires,

celebrities, people of moderate means, and poor folks down in the steerage. But a few hours later when they put the list in the Cunard office in New York, it carried only two categories—lost and saved. Grim tragedy had leveled all distinctions.[121]

Titanic certainly didn't universally abolish class discrimination, but it did cause society to see humanity without those categorizations for a brief time. To learn of the story of *Titanic*—whether in April 1912 or today—is to be reminded of one's own fragile mortality and that such a reality is unbounded by society's constructs of class. In her death, *Titanic* caused the world to examine its own hypocrisy in the *White Star Line*'s gross demonstration of such and remains a testament to the destruction that follows arrogance and division.

The anguishing story of *Titanic* had a profound impact on people all over the world even just based on the black and white newspaper reports. There were dramatic, empathetic responses from various corners of the globe, such as the Cabery, Illinois, man who so strongly connected with the trauma the men left aboard *Titanic* must have experienced that his subconscious reenacted the event. According to the *Portage Daily Register*, just a few weeks after *Titanic* sank, "Charles Coalthurst was discovered unconscious under his window, being seriously injured by a fall. Dreaming that he was on board the *Titanic*, he leaped to save women and children, and finally when the captain gave the word for all men to save themselves, he jumped head-first through the window, falling 15 feet."[122]

---

121 Vance Havner, *The Vance Havner Quotebook*, Dennis J. Hester, ed. (Michigan: Baker Publishing Group, 1986).
122 "Injured in *Titanic* Dream," *Portage Daily Register*, April 25, 1912, https://www.newspapers.com/image/611966031/?match=1&terms=%22Injured%20in%20Titanic%20Dream%22.

TITANIC, THE ETERNAL SHIP

Noël tried to put the ugly ordeal behind her—as did hundreds of others who survived *Titanic*—but the sensationalism around the sinking and, in particular, her role in guiding Lifeboat Number 8 to safety made it nearly impossible. News of the latest in inquiry proceedings and emerging theories of "what really happened" from lay people who caught reporters' ears kept *Titanic* alive in the media and public gatherings.

After Norman and Noël's return to Leslie House, England's *Newcastle Weekly Chronicle* printed the following account, called "The Countess and the Captain": "For his arms were about her now, his voice, eager and passionate, was in her ear. 'Countess . . . I had not meant to tell you, but you guessed, you knew I loved you.' The glowing face and happy radiant eyes were answer enough as their lips met."[123]

Luckily for Norman, the excerpt was just from a fictional romance written by Muriel C. Lindsay for the publication's weekly short story section, but the plot was obviously based on the accounts of Tom and Noël. It seemed that no matter where they went, survivors couldn't escape the fanfare of what had happened. The world was obsessed with all things *Titanic*, and Noël was among the most intriguing players in the saga.

Even if there had been no sensationalism surrounding *Titanic* at all, survivors needed no external reminders or triggers to visit *Titanic* often for the rest of their lives. *Titanic* may not have killed all aboard; but survivors all carried a similar chill in their bones

---

123 Muriel C. Lindsay, "The Countess and the Captain," *The Newcastle Weekly Chronicle*, November 2, 1912, https://www.newspapers.com/image/815081116/?match=1&terms=%22The%20Countess%20and%20the%20Captain%22.

that lasted a lifetime, though it was something they dared not mention. The world didn't have a well-established understanding of Post-traumatic Stress Disorder at the time of *Titanic*'s sinking, but it is safe to assume that all *Titanic* survivors surely had some degree of the condition, including Noël.

PTSD is now widely understood through troubling mental health symptoms, such as nightmares, flashbacks, and varying degrees of anxiety subsequent to a traumatic event or series of events. In the early 1900s, mental health studies were not in their most progressive phases; and many physicians would simply give a flippant diagnosis of "nerves" or "nervous disorder" to a patient following some terrible occurrence in their life. Other physicians of Noël's era; however, never had the opportunity to diagnose such a condition at all because patients were too ashamed of their symptoms to report them. Today, PTSD is a societally accepted diagnosis that is often met with understanding and compassion that was non-existent when *Titanic* survivors came under the influence of their own post-traumatic stress conditions. They simply suffered the complexities of their symptoms (that sometimes lasted entire lifetimes) in stoic silence.

Just a year after the harrowing night on the sea of glass, Noël was dining with friends of aristocracy in a sumptuous London restaurant when a flashback overtook her. Though the earl in tails looking at her through soft candlelight had no resemblance to Tom Jones in his seaman's hat and lifebelt and the soft murmur of the crowd had no tinges of watery screams, Noël found herself back in Lifeboat Number 8. The dreadful time machine had been activated by the London restaurant's orchestra's selection of the

"Tales of Hoffman" song played the night of April 14 by Wally Hartley's men as *Titanic*'s first-class passengers concluded their last dinner aboard the great liner.

Years later, Noël described the flashback to author Walter Lord for his book *A Night to Remember* as "the awful feeling of cold and intense horror."[124] Surely, those frightening, nameless feelings lingered in waves of duality: great fear and great grief. In a certain way, despite those who survived physically, everyone who boarded *Titanic* on April 10, 1912, never left.

GOD HIMSELF

With what the world pieced together as the *Titanic* narrative came more questions than answers, no matter how many inquiries were held. Outlandish fringe explanations emerged into public chatter through gossip or media that contained sprigs of spiritualism or superstition. Some believed the *White Star Line* to be cursed because they broke from the tradition and did not christen their ships. Others agreed they were cursed—not with anything mystical but simply cursed with fleshly greed and pomposity that clouded reality to the demise of thousands.

The person or persons who supposedly made the infamous statement of "God Himself couldn't sink this ship" surely regretted the narrow-sighted boast after what happened. That statement had the pride knocked out of it in those horrific last moments of thousands, and it was shortened to simply, "God Himself," for that was their only hope amid the dark and motionless abyss.

---

124 Lord, *A Night to Remember*, 159.

One of the survivors who went on to give several different interviews about the disaster throughout her lifetime was Eva Hart. She was seven years old when she sailed on *Titanic* with her parents, Benjamin and Esther Hart. As a devout Christian, Esther had a dreadful premonition of doom that only grew stronger the more she heard talk of the ship being "unsinkable." Eva recalled that her mother refused to sleep at night aboard *Titanic*. So strong were her convictions that no ship should be called unsinkable, she would sleep in the daytime and knit and read through the nighttime hours. Esther believed the claims that "even God himself couldn't sink this ship" were blasphemous and flew in the face of the Holy God. Esther and Eva survived the disaster, while Benjamin was among the lost. Esther recalled, "I can honestly say that from the moment the journey to Canada was mentioned till the time we got aboard *Titanic*, I never contemplated with any other feelings but those of dread and uneasiness."[125]

The priest and atheist alike found their knees that evening, even if the floor they knelt on was the ocean floor. The Sovereign God was what thousands clung to when Greek mythology and man's arrogance had failed. In *Titanic* survivor Lawrence Beesley's book, *The Loss of the S.S. Titanic: Its Story and Its Lessons*, he recalled:

> The story may or may not be true, and in any case is not introduced as an attack on atheism, but it illustrates in a striking way the frailty of dependence on a man's own power and resource in imminent danger. To those men standing on the top deck with the boats all lowered, and still more so when the boats had all left, there came the

---

[125] Bancroft, 47.

realization that human resources were exhausted and human avenues of escape closed. With it came the appeal to whatever consciousness each had of a Power that had created the universe. After all, some Power had made the brilliant stars above, countless millions of miles away, moving in definite order, formed on a definite plan and obeying a definite law: had made each one of the passengers with ability to think and act; with the best proof, after all, of being created—the knowledge of their own existence; and now, if at any time, was the time to appeal to that Power. When the boats had left and it was seen the ship was going down rapidly, men stood in groups on the deck engaged in prayer, and later, as some of them lay on the overturned collapsible boat, they repeated together over and over again the Lord's Prayer—irrespective of religious beliefs, some, perhaps, without religious beliefs, united in a common appeal for deliverance from their surroundings. And this was not because it was a habit, because they had learned this prayer "at their mother's knee": men do not do such things through habit. It must have been because each one saw removed the thousand and one ways in which he had relied on human, material things to help him—including even dependence on the overturned boat with its bubble of air inside, which any moment a rising swell might remove as it tilted the boat too far sideways, and sink the boat below the surface—saw laid bare his utter dependence on something that had made him and given him power to think—whether he named it God or Divine Power or First Cause or Creator, or named it not at all but recognized it unconsciously—saw these things and expressed them in the form of words he was best acquainted with in common with his fellow-men. He did so, not through a sense of duty to his particular religion, not because he had learned the words, but because he recognized that it was the most practical thing to do—the thing best fitted to help him. Men do practical things in times like that: they would not waste a moment on mere words if those words were not an expression of the most intensely real conviction of which they were capable. Again, like the feeling of heroism, this appeal is innate and intuitive, and it certainly has its foundation on a knowledge—largely concealed, no doubt—of immortality. I think this must be obvious: there could be no other explanation of such a general sinking of all the emotions of the human mind expressed in a thousand different ways by a thousand different people in favour of this single appeal.[126]

Of course, there were hundreds of "I told you so" moments that clamored loudly about pubs and newspapers in the aftermath. Newspapers reported batches of stories of confirmatory bias that many "just knew" *Titanic* would sink through nighttime visions, daytime premonitions, or just the general sense of "doom" that surrounded the ship. These people claimed they never for a moment believed the "unsinkable" gimmick and looked upon anyone who did a fool.

Those stories are always fascinating—and some are surely true—but the great tragedy of the thing is that *Titanic*'s glory shielded any catchable hints of mishap, making her story all the more tragic. Many of the "omens" people subsequently claimed to have were just natural human responses in trying to make sense of such disaster in worldwide grief. There were thousands

---

126 Lawrence Beesley, *The Loss of the S.S. Titanic: Its Story and Its Lessons* (Boston, MA: Mariner Books, 2000), 294.

of reports of "foreboding" feelings, strange coincidences, superstitions, curses, and unexplained circumstances surrounding *Titanic* and her passengers. Traumatic events never get retold with cohesion, especially when thousands of people experience the same event. Those perceived gaps caused by different interpretations of different dimensions of the same tragic event may be one of the reasons why there are so many "holes" in the story that we still long to fill with speculation and more information, though there is no more that can change the finality of the end of *Titanic*'s story. The "might have beens" of *Titanic* are difficult to contend with. As *Titanic* historian Walter Lord said:

> What troubled people especially was not just the tragedy—or even its needlessness—but the element of fate in it all. If the *Titanic* had heeded any of the six ice messages on Sunday . . . if ice conditions had been normal . . . if the night had been rough or moonlit . . . if she had seen the berg 15 seconds sooner—or 15 seconds later . . . if she had hit the ice any other way . . . if her watertight bulkheads had been one deck higher . . . if she had carried enough boats . . . if the *Californian* had only come. Had any one of these "ifs" turned out right, every life might have been saved. But they all went against her—a classic Greek tragedy.[127]

TOM

Despite the catastrophe, Able Seaman Tom Jones continued his work on the fickle seas. In June 1912, a letter that the countess's

---

127 Lord, *A Night to Remember*, 149.

cousin-in-law, Gladys Cherry, had written to Tom somehow found its way into England's newspapers:

> I feel I must write and tell you how splendidly you took charge of our boat on the fatal night. There were only four English people in it—my cousin Lady Rothes, her maid, you, and myself—and I think you were wonderful. The dreadful regret I shall always have and I know you share with me, is that we ought to have gone back to see whom we could pick up. But if you remember there was only an American lady, my cousin, self, and you who wanted to return. I could not hear the discussion very clearly, as I was at the tiller, but everyone forward, and the three men refused. But I shall always remember your words, "Ladies, if any of us are saved, remember I wanted to go back. I would rather drown with them than leave them." You did all you could, and being my own countryman, I wanted to tell you this. -Yours, very truly, Gladys Cherry.[128]

For their courage and care of passengers in Lifeboat Number 8 on that April night, the countess sent Tom and Steward Alfred Crawford each an engraved fob watch with the inscription: *April 15th, 1912, The Countess of Rothes*. It became Tom's prized possession, and he wrote her the following thanks:

> My Lady,
>
> I have only today received your very gracious present, and I appreciate, very much, the honour extended

---

128 Gladys Cherry, "A Remarkable Letter," *The Daily Telegraph*, May 27, 1912, https://www.newspapers.com/image/818671595/?match=1&terms=%22I%20feel%20I%20must%20write%20and%20tell%20you%20how%22.

to me by your Grace in acknowledging any service rendered by me at the time of the disaster—which was my duty to those of whom I was in charge. May I say how much service you rendered myself and others by your example and courage under so heart-rending circumstances.

I shall always treasure your kind gift as my priceless possession. I have the honour to be Your Grace's obedient servant,

T Jones[129]

To memorialize the countess' own heroism at the tiller and oars, in September of 1912, Tom sent Noël a round, wooden plaque with one of the bronze eights cut from the side of Lifeboat Number 8 along with the following letter:

My Lady,

I beg to ask your acceptance of the number of my boat from which you were taken on board *SS Carpathia*.

This number is the original taken from the boat by myself. In asking you to accept the same I do so in respect for your courage under so terrifying circumstances.

Trusting you are now fully recovered to health,

I am,

Your obedient servant,

Tom Jones A.B. Late *SS Titanic*.[130]

---

[129] Tom Jones, "Letter to Countess," *Encyclopedia-Titanica*, accessed January 18, 2024, https://www.encyclopedia-titanica.org/titanic-survivor/thomas-william-jones.html.

[130] Ibid.

Tom married Clara Moulton in 1916, and they went on to have three children. Their only son, William, followed in his father's seaman footsteps; but at the age of twenty-one, William was killed in 1940 when the *SS Samala* was torpedoed en route from Jamaica to Britain.[131]

There have been innuendos of romantic tensions between Tom and Noël as their story has been passed down; but if those tensions existed at all, they weren't to be acted upon by either. If either fell in love, surely, it was incited by the primal urges to simply survive that night upon the water that tangled themselves in the heroism of the other. But the world loves a love story, and the dainty lady of nobility falling for the unlikely rugged seaman makes for an intriguing undercurrent of Tom and Noël.

Tom died in 1967 at the age of eighty-nine after a long, full life and complex love affair with the sea. He and Noël remained in contact until her death eleven years before his own. They shouldered each other along in spirit and correspondence for over forty years after their unforgettable night together that they both feared would be their last.

Tom's daughter, Ellen Jones, recalled him as "a lovely dad" of whom she was and is very proud.[132] She also recalled how a Christmas never went by after *Titanic* that her father didn't receive a letter from the countess with a pound inside.

---

131 "Thomas William Jones: RMS *Titanic* Able Seaman," *Encyclopedia-Titanica*. Accessed November 14, 2023. https://www.encyclopedia-titanica.org/titanic-survivor/thomas-william-jones.html.
132 Ellen Jones, "*Titanic*: Unlikely Friendship in Lifeboat Eight," *BBC News*, April 14, 2012, https://www.bbc.co.uk/news/uk-england-17583924.

SOCIAL SEASONS AND WAR

Noël went on in life, just as the other survivors did, carrying the invisible wounds that lasted long beyond the blistered hands and frostbitten feet. She continued to travel the globe much as she had before, though the secret residuals gripped her on occasion in all the "what ifs" that *Titanic* trauma never stopped asking. One of the heaviest of those residuals was the survivor guilt of not having been able to go back for more people in the water. The pleas of the hundreds they couldn't save haunted Noël beyond description. She carried their shouts and bobbing shadows with her to her deathbed.

The suffocating regret Noël had was something she occasionally spoke of to Norman and her parents, as it was a consuming feeling difficult to keep completely concealed. Despite earning celebrity of an unexpected kind after April 15, 1912, Noël went on in her noble title and all it required. She happily resumed her motherly role with John and Malcolm, who, by 1912, had been under a doctor's care for an extended illness.

By late 1913, Noël resumed many of her former engagements and accepted a few new ones, though her momentum waned after *Titanic*. In place of the extravagant banquets held at Leslie House with Noël hosting, she preferred quieter, simpler gatherings at their London townhome.

Through 1914, she elected for behind-the-scenes contributions to the social season instead of her usual festive presence at garden parties, charity balls, and political fundraisers. The appearances she did make were just as delicately radiant as ever, but her capacity for the porcelain affairs of the upper-class had waned since seeing the world from Lifeboat Number 8. After having been eye to eye with icy death, small-talk critiques of bouillon consistency and rose form seemed more frivolous than they ever had to Noël. The whispers and lengthy glances she had always received from crowds for her beauty had doubled with the "expert oarswoman" reputation she had earned through the newspapers. She showed no signs of having ever been a seaman, making her all the more curious to others of all classes who caught a glimpse of the "plucky little countess."

The Home Rule Bill that had so divided Lord Pirrie's shipyard men during the construction of the *Olympic*-class sisters passed through Parliament in 1914 after a two-year tussle. The countess had vehemently opposed the bill and poured significant personal emotional and financial investment into preventing its parliament passage.

At the same time, other political tensions were mounting throughout Europe and finally reached their bloody pitch on June 28, 1914, when Austria-Hungarian Archduke Franz Ferdinand and his wife, Sophie Chotek, were assassinated by Gavrilo Princip, a Bosnian Serb nationalist. Their deaths ignited a chain of defensive events that erupted into the First World War.[133]

In August 1914, under George V's rule, Britain officially entered the fight after Germany's invasion of Belgium. The world thundered in war for four crimson years, and more than twenty million people became casualties. On the other side of such devastation came the end of the Edwardian Era.

---

133 Tim Butcher, *The Trigger: Hunting the Assassin Who Brought the World to War* (New York City, NY: Grove Press, 2014), 89.

CHAPTER SIX
Later Years and Legacy

"It is a fascinating story. [Noël] was a typical product of the period and displayed a very British stiff upper lip in the face of adversity. She set a marvellous[sic] example to those around her."[134]

Noël was only thirty-two years old when she manned Lifeboat Number 8, and there were decades more to her story after *Titanic* that proved just as daring and selfless but perhaps not as publicized. With the outbreak of World War I, she and Norman were both called to the frontlines in their respective roles.

True to his Scottish representative peer election in 1906 and his title of earl, Norman remained thoroughly abreast of world socioeconomic and political conditions; so it was no surprise to him when Britain declared war on Germany. Swallowing a whole history of tensions, Scotland joined Britain along with France, Italy, Canada, Japan, Romania, Russia, and the United States in

---

134 Father Fabian, "The Countess Who Became Heroine of the *Titanic*," *Western Daily Press*, January 30, 1998, https://www.newspapers.com/image/921936192/?match=1&terms=%22Like%20an%20earthquake%20or%20a%20distant%20battle%22.

the fight against the Central Powers of Bulgaria, Austria-Hungary, the Ottoman Empire, and, of course, Germany. Norman was one of the roughly 190,000 Scottish men to volunteer before the 1916 draft, and he served with the Highland Cyclist Battalion as lieutenant-colonel and with the Black Watch, 3rd Battalion, Royal Regiment of Scotland first in St. Andrews, Scotland.[135]

In continuing her work with Scotland's Red Cross initiatives, Noël led efforts to establish hospital sites throughout the country's churches; but having no adequate prospects for an overflow Fife campus without constructing a brand-new building, she offered Leslie House as Fife's medic central.

Though Norman's Fife command headquarters was initially only about thirty miles from Leslie House, he was ultimately sent to frontline theaters in France. Before he left home, Norman helped Noël convert their estate into a hospital and safe haven for the growing number of Belgian refugees who had made their way to the shores of Scotland to escape Central Power domination. Norman even had a communications system installed in the library of Leslie House to provide Noël and her team a direct telephone line to Scotland's command centers.

Noël didn't just nonchalantly offer her home to the war relief effort and hole up in her velvet-trimmed chamber suite. She did exactly what she had done aboard *Carpathia* in moving expeditiously about the various sick bays offering what food, clothing, and hands-on medical care she could. She personally

---

[135] "The Earl of Rothes," *The Gloucestershire Echo*, March 30, 1927, https://www.newspapers.com/image/798744542/?match=1&terms=%22The%20Earl%20of%20Rothes%22.

managed a team of floor nurses and steadily worked alongside them in the care of the wounded and dying.

Noël had served with the Red Cross since long before *Titanic*, but being able to serve with them again in such a hands-on way was therapeutic for her in a way it hadn't been before. She found greater purpose in having her nursing skills be of use as some personal retribution given to those she couldn't save from the North Atlantic years before. While no one relished the world's dire circumstances in World War I, Noël was pleased she could be of some immediate assistance in the thick of such warfare. She also leveraged her hostess expertise in organizing bazaars to aid the French Wounded Emergency Fund. Noël and her teams of all classes sold flowers to raise money for medical supplies and, in some cases, funeral costs for the nearly seven thousand French hospitals caring for wounded soldiers and civilians.[136]

In the fall of 1915, Noël's father, Thomas, saw a need amid the war that he could meet on Noël's behalf. One year after Britain joined the fight, Thomas gifted the town of Fraserburgh, Scotland, a lifeboat and christened it *Lady Rothes* in honor of Noël. He said the donation "was a thanks-offering to Almighty God for the safety of his only child from the wreck of the *Titanic*."[137] Before the public ceremony, Noël vehemently forbade her father to mention anything about her rowing in Lifeboat Number 8. *The Gloucester Journal* reported:

> A large number of ladies and gentlemen availed themselves of the invitation to go on board the lifeboat prior to the launch. Lady Rothes then went

---

136 Bigham, *A Matter of Course*.
137 *The Gloucestershire Echo,* July 17, 1915, https://www.newspapers.com/image/798684703/?match=1&terms=titanic.

to the bow of the vessel, against which she broke a bottle of wine and said, "I christen this boat *Lady Rothes*," amid loud cheers. Miss Finlayson presented her ladyship with a beautiful bouquet. Lady Rothes accompanied by her father and her husband, Lord Rothes, who wore the uniform of Colonel of the Highland Cyclists' Battalion attached to the Black Watch joined the company on board. Coxswain Andrew Noble took his place at the helm, and amid ringing cheers the *Lady Rothes* slipped gracefully into the water and left the harbour for a short cruise in the bay.[138]

In part, *Lady Rothes* was a redemptive gift for Noël as much as it was a useful one for the people of Fraserburgh. Thomas wanted to help ease Noël's *Titanic* survivor's guilt by giving her name the opportunity to rescue others caught up in the billows of the North Sea. Noël reveled in the reports of *Lady Rothes'* role in rescue efforts, for her years on the water during wartime when the vessel carried many to safe shores.

WOUNDS ON THE FRONTLINES

Norman always insisted the trenches he was in were far removed from any real danger, but Noël's intuition suspected otherwise. Her suspicions were terribly confirmed when Norman was listed in the papers among the severely wounded when flying shrapnel caused him facial and leg injuries in 1916. He had recovered from his wounds almost before Noël first learned of

---

[138] "Mr. T Dyer-Edwardes' Thank-Offering," *The Gloucester Journal*, August 14, 1915.

them, and Norman was back in the trenches of France within a few days.[139]

The next year, however, Norman suffered even more severe injuries while fighting alongside his company when shrapnel took one of his eyes. He was transported to London's Coulter Hospital, where he remained for several months undergoing a series of surgeries. Noël left Leslie House and rushed to his side, becoming his exclusive nurse until he was well enough to return home. In her absence, a teenaged Malcolm was head of the house and managed many of his parents' duties while they were away. On November 14, 1917, Lieutenant-Colonel N.E. Earl of Rothes relinquished his appointment due to his injuries.[140]

In July 1918, just a few months before World War I heaved to an end with Germany signing an armistice, *Lead Kindly, Light* recurred in Noël's life as *Titanic* historian Randy Bryan Bigham describes:

> Noëlle participated in a special jewelry exhibition at the Grafton Galleries. Benefiting the Red Cross, the show celebrated "the beauty and history of the pearl," with magnificent donations from Queen Alexandra, Princess Mary (the Princess Royal) and other notables. Among the many examples, arranged singly and in pairs, that went on view were two superb pearls selected by Noëlle from the centuries-old necklace she wore the night *Titanic* sank. Displayed in a case framed in royal blue silk, the Countess' pearls were suspended from a slim satin ribbon on a cream velvet

---

139 "Norman Evelyn Leslie, 19th Earl of Rothes," The Peerage, accessed November 7, 2023, https://www.thepeerage.com/p8538.htm#i85377.
140 "Local Commissions," The Gloucester Journal, December 22, 1917, https://www.newspapers.com/image/793739866/?match=1&terms=%22earl%20of%20rothes%22.

pillow. Fully described in the exhibition catalogue, their "ancient and recent history" was also given in the programme under the heading "Lead, Kindly Light," after the hymn their "noble owner sang as she pulled an oar in her lifeboat."[141]

As much as Noël appreciated the continued commemoration of her Lifeboat Number 8 heroism, *Titanic* seemed to cast an immovable shadow on her efforts to move on from the tragedy. One of the ways she dealt with the ship-shaped shadow was to continue plunging back into her work with the Red Cross. She continued in Red Cross satellite site launches in London through 1918, as wounded soldiers and civilians continued overflowing established medical resources.

Norman carried war fatigue and his physical wounds with him for the rest of his life. When the war ended, the world's economy steadily trickled into recession; and Norman and Noël found themselves in unfamiliar financial territory. With Norman's war injuries, he was unable to return to the plethora of duties his nobility required; and the reserves of the Rothes synchronously declined with the world's economy. Norman and Noël were forced to adjust their sails accordingly.

AFTER WAR

On April 28, 1919, Noël found herself grieving another maritime disaster. After a distress call was received from the ship *Eminent* off the coast of Fraserburgh Bay, the lifeboat *Lady Rothes* was dispatched to her aid. Coxswain Andrew Noble, who had

---

141 Bigham, *A Matter of Course.*

been present when Noël christened *Lady Rothes* in 1915, and Acting Second Coxswain Andrew Farquhar commanded the boat with eleven crew aboard. As *Lady Rothes* sailed toward the ailing ship, whose engine had broken down, crowds gathered at the edge of the bay to watch the rescue. A gale caught the lifeboat from the Northeast. Just before she reached *Eminent*, one wave knocked the lifeboat sideways; and a second wave capsized her completely. Ten of the thirteen men aboard were pulled into the water, and only eight survived. The boat was righted, and most of the crew made it to shore after much struggle against the North Sea conditions, but several remained in the water until hoisted out by people from the harbor. Andrew Noble and Andrew Farquhar were two of the men pulled from the surf, but they died soon after from exposure. The *Eminent* ran aground shortly after, and all of her nine crew members were saved.[142]

Noël was devastated upon hearing *Lady Rothes* had not only failed to save those she was sent to but had taken two lives in the process, one of which she considered a friend. Despite Norman and Noël's precarious financial situation, Noël provided financial support to the widows and children of both Andrews; and after repair, *Lady Rothes* went on in her service for another eighteen years until she was officially retired in 1937.[143]

Today, there stands the Fraserburgh Lifeboat Memorial in commemoration of Andrew Noble and Andrew Farquhar and eleven other men who lost their lives in separate, subsequent

---

142 "Fraserburgh, 1919: A Capsized Crew in a Courageous Community," *Lifeboats RNLI* 200, April 25, 2019, https://rnli.org/magazine/magazine-featured-list/2019/april/fraserburgh-capsized-crew.
143 Ibid.

Fraserburgh lifeboat disasters with the inscription: "Greater love hath no man than this, that he lay down his life for his fellow man."[144]

In the summer of 1919, the Rothes were faced with impossible decisions with the dwindling of their finances; their future outlook had only grown dimmer since the onset of Norman's failing health. Together, they decided to sell their beloved Leslie House and move into their smaller, more manageable townhouse in Chelsea, London.[145] With Fife's long-celebrated estate home went its furnishings and the remaining thirty-five hundred acres. Shalden's Captain Alexander Crundall purchased Leslie House, and Norman and Noël had the difficult task of breaking the news to their tenants and Leslie community. Throngs of Fife's townspeople came together in petitioning the Rothes to abandon their plans to move and remain in the region, even if Leslie House did have to sell. Norman and Noël were tremendously touched by the gesture but made arrangements to move back to London by September of that year. Though their petition had failed, the people of Leslie swarmed the town hall in an emotional farewell celebration honoring the couple for their years of selfless care to love, unify, and grow Leslie.

Since 1904, when Norman's great uncle, the Hon. George Waldegrave Leslie, bequeathed the estate to him, Norman and Noël had considered those of Leslie, Fife, their family, regardless of class; and leaving them behind was one of the worst parts of their financial collapse. The marbled vanities and mahogany settees were naturally

---
144 Ibid.
145 "Lord Rothes Puts His Estate in Scotland on the Market," *The Washington Post*, July 19, 1919.

hard to part with, but nothing compared to leaving Leslie's people and the years of memories behind. The townspeople saw them off with tears and waving handkerchiefs. Noël was presented with a hand-crafted gold bracelet and Norman with an imperial onyx cup lined with silver gilt. They treasured these memorials of their Scotland people for the rest of their lives.

Norman and Noël settled into a small existence in London nearer Thomas and Clementina. In their forties by 1920, Norman and Noël were empty-nesters as their sons, Malcolm and John, had begun their own journeys toward the same well-received philanthropic presence in the aristocratic society their parents had maintained for years. Norman maintained many of his duties as representative peer for Scotland until the early 1920s when Malcolm was eligible to succeed him.

A DIFFERENT CHAPTER

On February 2, 1926, at the age of seventy-nine, Noël's father, Thomas Dyer-Edwardes died suddenly of a heart attack while on a visit to Naples, Italy.[146] Because of his later-in-life conversion to Catholicism, there had been significant rifts in the family dynamics. Many of his family members, including Clementina, clung tightly to their Anglican beliefs in firm allegiance to the Church of England and thought Thomas a traitor in his decision to convert. So sincerely did he convert to the Roman Catholic Church in the early 1920s that he offered to gift the Catholic Benedictines

---

146 "Death of Mr. T. Dyer-Edwardes," The Citizen, February 12, 1926, https://www.newspapers.com/image/792093987/?match=1&terms=edwardes.

of Caldy Island, Wales, their Prinknash Park residence. Thomas wrote to Bishop Arthur Headlam through a liaison:

> I am now writing you to ask if you could approach the Bishop of Gloucester as I do not know him personally with a view of sounding him as to making Prinknash a house of retreat for Clergy or for a Community? The house, its history and surroundings has always appeared to me so admirable for such a purpose. The house, grounds, kitchen garden and stables, in all about 14 acres, run into about 300 a year; it is assessed at that. I would let the house and grounds free of rent from year to year on a six months' notice.[147]

Prinknash Park is steeped in Benedictine tradition as the host of a sixteenth-century abbey, Thomas' decision to bequeath his Prinknash home to the current order of Benedictine monks wasn't so far removed from its history. His abrupt and more-than-generous offer to the order led to tumultuous back-and-forth negotiations in the legalities of how and when the community of monks could accept. It also led to tumultuous back-and-forth arguments with Clementina, and the two divorced over the matter after forty-six years of marriage.[148]

Thomas died before the Benedictine order could rightfully accept Prinknash Park, and the estate and its fourteen acres went to Malcolm Leslie. In 1928, however, Malcolm honored his grandfather's wishes and completed the process of signing over

---

147 "Prinknash Park: Owner's Offer Not Accepted by Bishop Gloucester," *The Citizen*, January 2, 1926, https://www.newspapers.com/image/792089032/?match=1&terms=%22Bishop%20of%20Gloucester%22.
148 Bigham, *A Matter of Course*.

ownership of Prinknash Park to the Caldy Benedictines.¹⁴⁹ It is still maintained as a Roman Catholic monastery today.

Like so many millions who served, Norman never quite recovered from the war emotionally or physically. Despite his many surgeries and the excellent nursing care Noël had given so tenderly at his bedside, his health declined rapidly after parting with beloved Leslie House. Noël persisted in her philanthropic efforts nearly exclusive to England after she and Norman settled in Chelsea. While Noël still turned out for the British social season in her exclusive gowns of satin and extravagant hats by fellow *Titanic* survivor Lady Duff Gordon, she did so without Norman, who, by 1927, had become nearly bedridden. At the age of forty-nine, the earl died on March 29, 1927, at Mortimer, Berkshire, with his lovely countess of twenty-seven years at his bedside.¹⁵⁰

By 1927, Malcolm Leslie was a handsome man of distinction as a mirror of his father in good looks and diplomacy. He married Beryl Violet Dugdale after graduating from Windsor's Eton College and became the twentieth Earl of Rothes upon his father's death. Malcolm went on his Representative Peer of Scotland duties as well and became chairman of the National Mutual Life Assurance Society. He and Beryl had three children: Lady Jean Leslie, Lady Evelyn Leslie, and Ian Lionel Malcolm Leslie, who eventually succeeded his father as the twenty-first Earl of Rothes.¹⁵¹

---

149 "A Romantic Isle," *The Manchester Evening News*, September 29, 1928, https://www.newspapers.com/image/937825394/?match=1&terms=%22Prinknash%20Park%22.
150 "The Earl of Rothes," *The Gloucestershire Echo*, March 30, 1927, https://www.newspapers.com/image/798744542/?match=1&terms=%22The%20Earl%20of%20Rothes%22.
151 "Norman Evelyn Leslie, 19th Earl of Rothes," The Peerage, accessed November 7, 2023, https://www.thepeerage.com/p8538.htm#i85377.

The much younger John was studying at the University of Cambridge when his father died. As second in line for earl, he followed in his father's military footsteps and joined Scotland's Royal Company of Archers, earned the rank of flight lieutenant in the Royal Air Force Volunteer Reserve, and fought in World War II from 1939 until 1943, when he was severely injured and honorably discharged. John went on to marry Coral Angela Pinckard, and they had two children: Alastair Pinckard Leslie and Amber Elizabeth Leslie.[152]

NOËL MACFIE

Noël's sons were of great comfort to her in the mournful weeks and months that followed Thomas', and then Norman's, death. Malcolm and John each held distinctive features of their father and grandfather that reminded Noël of those early years of ease before the ravages of time, *Titanic*, war, and the sale of Leslie House. Norman was her heart's only true love, but they had lost each other somehow long before his physical death.

A friend of Norman's, the decorated British Colonel Claud Macfie, was also of great comfort to Noël in her widow's mourning. Claud was of a rich Scottish heritage but had been born in Lancashire, England, and joined the British infantry at a young age. When Claud and Noël became acquainted in London's social scene, he had been retired from command in the British Army's Seaforth Highlanders for several years and had a laudatory reputation among Britain's upper class. Like Norman,

---

[152] "Malcolm George Dyer-Edwardes Leslie, 20th Earl of Rothes," The Peerage, accessed November 8, 2023, https://www.thepeerage.com/p8539.htm#i85382.

Later Years and Legacy   143

he, too, had served bravely in the trenches of World War I and had the medals and battle scars to prove it. On December 22, 1927, Noël married Colonel Claud Macfie at the Holy Trinity Church in Chelsea, London; they both were forty-nine years old. Noël retained her title of nobility in honor of Norman, though she became Noël Leslie Macfie, Countess of Rothes.[153]

As a new bride, Noël moved with Claud into both of his residences, which were about 150 miles apart. He owned an estate in Fairford called Fayre Court and also had a more conservative home in Hove, Sussex. The two spent most of their time in their quiet country residence of Fayre Court, which was framed by rolling acres and bubbling streams of the River Coln.[154]

Despite her new settlements, Noël still continued in her work with the Red Cross and fostered new initiatives in and around Fairford. The social scene for the new Macfie couple was of very different sways than Noël had known with Norman. In Claud's retirement, he preferred a slower and steadier pace than the Leslies of Rothes had in their prime. As she aged, Noël appreciated the slower tempo Claud offered in their Fairford field strolls, sitting room readings, and intimate dinners with family and close friends. The days of royal banqueted affairs with straight-backed chiffon and twelve-courses had long passed.

Fayre Court was closer to Noël's mother's residence in Gloucestershire, and the two visited frequently in Clementina's

---

[153] "Betrothal of a Countess," *Cheltenham Chronicle and Gloucestershire Graphic*, December 24, 1927, https://www.newspapers.com/image/786270108/?match=1&terms=rothes.

[154] "The Countess Who Became Heroine of the *Titanic*," *Western Daily Press*, January 30, 1998, https://www.newspapers.com/image/921936192/?match=1&terms=%22Like%20an%20earthquake%20or%20a%20distant%20battle%22.

failing health. Clementina died on April 3, 1947, in the little town of Painswick at the age of eighty-eight.[155]

In her last years, Noël's tenacity never waned, but the slower pace of Fairford was a salve for the many years of turmoil that had followed *Titanic*. Not that *Titanic* caused all the trouble of course, but the sinking of the unsinkable did seem to be a catalyst for layers and layers of change in the lives of Noël and her fellow survivors, as well as the world itself.

In 1954, writer Walter Lord contacted Noël and more than sixty other *Titanic* survivors to collect their memories of the sinking for his book, *A Night to Remember*. It was a tedious process for Lord to track down survivors after so many years, arrange the meetings with them, and gather their traumatic eyewitness accounts; but it gave the world an up-close perspective of the disaster that we had not had before. The book was incredibly successful and led to Roy Ward Baker's 1958 film by the same name. The interview Noël gave to Lord was her first since arriving in New York just after the sinking when she sat for *The New York Herald*'s interview with Norman and Cissy. It would also be her last.

The timing of *Titanic* and the subsequent end of the Edwardian Era seemed to be a perfect storm that cascaded into trials of all kinds for both Norman and Noël. No one could ever begin to replace Norman and his fiery affections for his countess. Claud's was a more straightforward love with more straightforward manifestations that caused the two to age in a private, prosaic existence as the world around them began to shed the last of its traditional imperialism.

---

[155] "Deaths," *The Citizen*, April 5, 1947, https://www.newspapers.com/image/792863190/?match=1&terms=Clementina.

Noël had been approached by many writers and publications through the years who wanted to interview her as Walter Lord had in 1954 about *Titanic*, but she refused all requests. In 1956, publisher David Astor, who was a cousin of John Jacob Astor IV, of London's *The Observer* sent her an interview request. To Astor's happy surprise, she agreed.

Noël, as her father had, suffered from heart disease in her final years. She died peacefully in her sleep in Hove, Sussex on September 12, 1956, at the age of seventy-seven. Under Rev. Dr. D. B. Harris and Rev. D. C. Gray, a noon memorial was held for the countess at St. Paul's Knightsbridge. She was cremated at the Downs Crematorium, Brighton, Sussex, and her remains were laid with Norman in the Leslie Vault in Christ's Kirk on the Green Churchyard, Leslie, Fife, Scotland.[156]

Noël never met with David Astor for the *Titanic* interview, as she died the week of their scheduled meeting.[157] Though the ship is associated with the crux of Noël's legacy, she only ever gave two documented interviews about *Titanic*. Claud died the day after what would have been Noël's eighty-fourth birthday in 1963.

LEGACY

It has been almost seventy years since the countess left this world behind, yet her legacy continues in a multitude of ways. Because of her heroism on a harrowing April night in 1912, the countess and the world's most famous ship are eternally intertwined. The Countess

---

[156] "The Countess Who Became Heroine of the *Titanic*," *Western Daily Press*, January 30, 1998, https://www.newspapers.com/image/921936192/?match=1 &terms=%22Like%20an%20earthquake%20or%20a%20distant%20battle%22.
[157] Bigham, *A Matter of Course*.

of Rothes will forever be known as one of *Titanic*'s heroines in the chronicles of her "unsinkable" story.

Traces of Noël's less-publicized triumphs for humankind are found in the sociopolitical fabric of Britain and Scotland's twentieth century. Traces of her "scandalous" devotion to equality, unity, justice, and indiscriminate compassion are still evident in considering how she used the leverage of her noble platform not to selfishly indulge but to make the world better for others. The revered Christian virtues Noël espoused in her life's work can still be seen within the historical origins of women's suffrage, workers' union establishment, and class desegregation, along with her historic impact on the furtherance of the Red Cross and various hospital initiatives she helped establish throughout the United Kingdom.

Her beloved home in Leslie House changed hands numerous times after the Rothes sold it to Captain Crundall in 1919, eventually coming into the possession of Sir Robert Spencer Nairn as his private residence until 1952.[158] A few years before his death, Nairn gifted the property to the Church of Scotland. The Church converted Leslie House's main building into a convalescent facility, though in 2005, it was sold again—this time, to a development company that had plans to restore it. But during restoration efforts, in 2009, a fire destroyed much of the main home. Since then, Leslie House Development Company has purchased the property with plans to restore much of the original interior and convert the home into Scotland's history-honoring apartments.[159] Surely, Noël would be pleased in the efforts to

---

158 Bigham, *A Matter of Course*.
159 Claire Warrender, "Leslie House: Restoration Finally Under Way at the Home of *Titanic* Heroine," *The Courier Evening Telegraph*, September 9,

make practical use of and honorably preserve the grand Scottish grounds she and Norman so gingerly tended.

True to both the esteemed Leslie and Dyer-Edwardes clans, Norman and Noël's sons built similar altruistic legacies for themselves, as did their children and their grandchildren. The colorful stories of their family's "plucky little countess" have been passed down through the decades with great ancestral pride. As one of Noël's grandsons, Ian Rothes said of his grandmother in an interview with *Titanic* historian Randy Bryan Bigham not long before Ian's death, "She did exactly what anyone who knew her would have expected her to do . . . My grandmother approached daily life with that sort of determination. It may sound precious, but she always rowed for the light. Her religious faith directed her wherever she went."[160]

May we, too, have the pluck of the Countess of Rothes and persistently row for the light in all circumstances.

2021, https://www.thecourier.co.uk/fp/news/fife/2517314/leslie-house-restoration-finally-under-way-at-the-home-of-titanic-heroine.
160 Bigham, *A Matter of Course*.

Epilogue

The symbolism of *Titanic*, from her creation to her untimely foundering, has been examined and reexamined for more than one hundred years. We cannot know *Titanic* apart from her beginnings in arrogance that ultimately led her, and thousands who trusted in her, to their graves.

However mechanical our examination of this captivating story, all humans—whether Protestant, Catholic, spiritualist, atheist, or agnostic—eventually ask the same question in the tender coves of their hearts when closely considering *Titanic*: "But where was God?"

Along with their commentary on *Titanic* not long after the disaster, *The Omaha Daily Bee* printed a sketch of the ship of dreams steaming across the Atlantic with God's palm in place of the iceberg with the caption "the hollow of His hand." It's a stirring sketch but theologically all wrong. Because of the great storm of arrogance *Titanic* was developed and launched from, it's easy to view her fate through a quid-pro-quo lens. Humanity did this, so God did that; but that equation leaves no room for what God truly is: the loving Redeemer.

There are thousands of lessons and life parallels we can draw from *Titanic* as a cautionary tale. It has long since served as a parable on scales of all sizes. *Titanic* is used as a metaphor on all varieties of platforms from overreliance on technology to environmentalism to the Christian life and political agendas, but the crux is the same: great downfalls often follow great arrogance. This cause-and-effect is no mystery.

Did *Titanic* turn into a water grave just because someone flippantly said, "God Himself couldn't sink this ship?" I have no idea. I do know, however, that the same attitude behind that statement caused *Titanic*'s handlers to act recklessly at their posts in unnecessary speeding, failure to include enough lifeboats, refusal to heed ice warnings appropriately, and their general indifference to the actual collision and corresponding evacuation efforts. The true cautionary tale is found somewhere in those practical particulars, rather than in a wrathful God who was insulted by one singular ship of steel and iron.

God didn't have to sink *Titanic*. Man's arrogance did. There were multiple warnings and opportunities to avoid what happened from heeding the iceberg warnings to ensuring there were, indeed, enough lifeboats aboard. There was also the cloak of denial that had fallen over *White Star Line* employees, including Captain Smith, that a man-made vessel was impervious to everything, including human error. It's easier, and somehow more palatable, for us to comb through the reported omens of *Titanic*'s fate than for us to place the blame for her demise squarely on our own human arrogance. Arrogance can mean many different things depending on the context; but generally, the moral problem with arrogance is the division and recklessness it can cause, and *Titanic* is probably the most demonstrative example.

Titanic was never created to unite people or nations. She was created, from the beginning, to divide. She was created to set *White Star Line* apart from other ocean liner corporations, and she was created to maintain class and nationalistic division. She was a paragon of the Victorian and Edwardian Eras that kept the disadvantaged *more* disadvantaged and the advantaged *more* advantaged. *Titanic's* commanding officials were likewise caught up in that essence of arrogance *Titanic* was a product of, which ultimately led to their reckless handling of her and her passengers.

The antidote for the diabolical toxins of division and recklessness is what people like the Countess of Rothes had to offer that April night more than one hundred years ago. The countess was the antithesis of what sunk *Titanic*. She embodied humble nobility in selflessly tending to others. She courageously gave of herself with a stiff upper lip for her own troubles.

In the midst of mass destruction, the countess did not falter. She quietly led, soothed, and rowed for the lights. Her role in *Titanic* survivors' journey to safety was not loud and obvious. It did not repair *Titanic* or resurrect those who sank with her, but the graceful, intentional stepping down from first class to unite and lead others was, in my opinion, another tiny speck of God's redemptive presence that evening.

Titanic survivor Colonel Archibald Gracie said in his book, *The Truth About Titanic*: "God's part was the saving of the few souls on that calmest of oceans on that fearful night. Man's part was the pushing of the good ship, pushing against all reason."[161]

REDEMPTION

One of the millions of reasons the story of *Titanic* is such a captivating tale above many other maritime disasters is the inclination we as humans have toward redemption. *Titanic* is *not* a story of redemption; *Titanic* is a story of downfall. Humans are naturally wired for redemptive closure; and on the surface, *Titanic* gives us none. She was built. She sank upon her first time at sea. She will remain on the ocean floor for the rest of eternity. The injustice and finality of the story do not bode well with our innate desire for second chances, so we obsessively look for glimpses of redemption to satisfy that humanistic need for things to "make sense." And *Titanic* just doesn't. She was not supposed to sink. Our humanity is uncomfortable with her biography; so we metaphorically "raise her" in documentaries, movies, books, and reenactments to check again for traces of redemption. Despite modern capabilities our world now has to raise sunken shipwrecks, *Titanic* will never be one of those eligible for raising, experts tell us. In 1985, Robert Ballard found her for us, but no one has been able to raise her or duplicate her.

DIVISION AND RECKLESSNESS

The redemption of *Titanic* is in the footnotes of her ship-biography, in the quiet, fleeting stories of love and sacrifice

---

[161] Archibald Gracie, *The Truth About Titanic* (New York: Mitchell Kennerley, 1913), 255.

that so many of her passengers exhibited that awful night and afterward. The countess has gone down in history as one of the primary representatives of those "quiet and fleeting" traces of redemption in this story in living out the opposite of the division and recklessness that emanated from *White Star Line* and how they handled their ship of dreams.

UNITY AND CAREFULNESS

Titanic unified more people in her sinking than she ever did in her sailing. In the aftermath of the sinking, there was a multitude of representatives from every class and country that set aside their own nationalistic pride to respond. From worldwide memorial services to rescue efforts, there were few, if any, who said, "If *Titanic* is so mighty, let her save herself." Perhaps humans are more forgiving than the Atlantic is. *Titanic* survivor Colonel Archibald Gracie recalled in his book *The Truth About Titanic*:

> During all these struggles I had been uttering silent prayers for deliverance, and it occurred to me that this was the occasion of all others when we should join in an appeal to the Almighty as our last and only hope in life, and so it remained for one of these men, whom I had regarded as uncouth, a Roman Catholic seaman, to take precedence in suggesting the thought in the heart of everyone of us. He was astern and in arm's length of me. He first made inquiry as to the religion of each of us and found Episcopalians, Roman Catholics and Presbyterians. The suggestion that we should say the Lord's Prayer together met with instant approval, and our voices with one accord burst forth in repeating that great appeal to

the Creator [92] and Preserver of all mankind, and the only prayer that everyone of us knew and could unite in, thereby manifesting that we were all sons of God and brothers to each other whatever our sphere in life or creed might be. Recollections of this incident are embodied in my account as well as those of Bride and Thayer, independently reported in the New York papers on the morning after our arrival. This is what Bride recalls: "Somebody said 'don't the rest of you think we ought to pray?' The man who made the suggestion asked what the religion of the others was. Each man called out his religion. One was a Catholic, one a Methodist, one a Presbyterian. It was decided the most appropriate prayer for all of us was the Lord's Prayer. We spoke it over in chorus, with the man who first suggested that we pray as the leader."

Referring to this incident in his sermon on "The Lessons of the Great Disaster," the Rev. Dr. Newell Dwight Hillis, of Plymouth Church, says: "When Col. Gracie came up, after the sinking of the *Titanic*, he says that he made his way to a sunken raft. The submerged little raft was under water often, but every man, without regard to nationality, broke into instant prayer. There were many voices, but they all had one signification—their sole hope was [93] in God. There were no millionaires, for millions fell away like leaves; there were no poor; men were neither wise nor ignorant; they were simply human souls on the sinking raft; the night was black and the waves yeasty with foam, and the grave where the *Titanic* lay was silent under them, and the stars were silent over them! But as they prayed, each man by that inner light saw an invisible Friend walking across the waves. Henceforth, these need no books on Apologetics to prove there is a God. This man who has written his story tells us that God heard the prayers of some by giving them death, and heard the prayers of others equally by keeping them in life; but God alone is great!"

The lesson thus drawn from the incident described must be well appreciated by all my boatmates who realized the utter helplessness of our position, and that the only hope we then had in life was in our God, and as the Rev. Dr. Hillis says: "In that moment the evanescent, transient, temporary things dissolved like smoke, and the big, permanent things stood out—God, Truth, Purity, Love, and Oh! how happy those who were good friends with God, their conscience and their record."[162]

A heroic *Titanic* figure similar to Noël in that fleeting redemption was the Scottish Baptist minister John Harper. Born in Houston, Renfrewshire, Scotland, in 1872, Harper became a Christian at an early age and felt the call of ministry at eighteen. He worked as a mill laborer in Scotland and would guest preach on Sundays in his community until a London pastor recruited him for full-time ministry in Govan.

Harper was the first pastor of Paisley Road Baptist Church in Glasgow, Scotland, which was only about sixty miles from Leslie House, so perhaps he and Noël had met in their mutual support

---

162 Ibid, 91.

of church charity long before they both boarded *Titanic*. Harper grew the little church in Glasgow from a congregation of twenty-five members to more than five hundred, which caused the need for a newer and larger location. In his honor, the church's new building was renamed Harper Memorial Baptist Church. Today, the church is called Harper Church with a large, thriving congregation of modern means in both Glasgow and Govan with a gospel-spreading vision much like John Harper's.

After accepting the full-time preaching engagement John Harper married and had a daughter, though his wife, Annie, died young, leaving him to raise little Nana on his own. He traveled the world in his ministry and earned a luminary reputation for winning souls to Christ. By the age of thirty-nine, he had preached nearly all over the globe and tirelessly lived out what he believed. As his biographer Moody Adams said, "[John Harper] lived and preached as if Christ died yesterday, rose today, and was coming tomorrow."[163]

In 1912, Harper had an opportunity to preach again at Chicago's Moody Church so he and his daughter, Nana, and his niece boarded *Titanic* to make the voyage to America. When disaster struck, Harper was reportedly unfazed. He first saw Nana and his niece to safety aboard a lifeboat and then remained aboard the doomed ship to lead others to Christ before they entered their graves. There are numerous reports of how he prayed, sang, and recited Scripture with fellow passengers as *Titanic* sank lower and lower into the black waters. One of the most well-known

---

[163] Moody Adams, *The Titanic's Last Hero: A Startling True Story That Can Change Your Life Forever* (Belfast: Ambassador International, 2012), 87.

anecdotes of Harper's final moments on earth is his exchange with a man who refused the offer of Christ as he and Harper's shoes began to disappear beneath the ocean's surface along with the deck. Harper asked the man again if he would come to Christ; and again, the man refused. Finally, Harper took his own life vest off, put it on the man, and said, "Very well, then you need this more than I do."[164]

Survivor George Henry Cavell claimed to be Harper's very last convert as they both struggled with the stabs of ice daggers in the water after they were swept from the deck. With John Harper's literal last breath, he led Cavell to Christ and then sank in frozen death to the depths. Cavell was subsequently picked up by one of the lifeboats that came back and testified of Harper's great faith and bravery that forever changed his life.

John Harper's own pluck was similar to the countess', as they both lived to unify and carefully tended to those around them in an era that was known for the very opposite. In the end, both Harper and the countess loved as Christ loved in offering the antidote for the division and recklessness of the world. Those principles are just as poignant today as they were more than one hundred years ago.

As John Harper's biographer, Moody Adams said:

> Following the sinking of the *Titanic*, the White Star office in Liverpool, England, placed a large board on either side of the main entrance. On one they printed in large letters: "KNOWN TO BE SAVED." On

---

[164] Douglas W. Mize, "As *Titanic* Sank, He Pleaded, 'Believe in the Lord Jesus!'" *Baptist Press*, April 13, 2012, https://www.baptistpress.com/resource-library/news/as-titanic-sank-he-pleaded-believe-in-the-lord-jesus.

the other, "KNOWN TO BE LOST." When *Titanic*'s voyage began, there were three classes of passengers. But when it ended, the number was reduced to only two—those who were "saved" by the rescue boats and those who were "lost" in the deep waters.[165]

The year before *Titanic* sank, John Harper delivered a sermon at Chicago's Moody Church that began:

> Vision, compassion, intercession—these are three great links in the golden chain of redemptive service. How clearly you can see them in the saving ministry and life service of our Lord Jesus Himself. He saw the multitudes as sheep without a shepherd—scattered, torn, bruised, and bleeding—and if that was the vision before His eyes when He looked on a multitude from the quiet religious village of Galilee, where the people were moral in their habits of life and sunken with drink and manifold vice, what would be the vision before Him if He looked today on Chicago?
>
> With that vision, His heart was moved with compassion, agitated with deep feeling—agonized within Him would be a better word. He had compassion on them, taking their pain and sorrow up into His own heart of love, and with that love-swept spirit He turns to His disciples and says, "Pray ye." On every possible occasion, He slips off Himself to the lonely mountainside to spend the night or early morning hours in prayer.[166]

---

[165] Adams, *The Titanic's Last Hero: A Startling True Story That Can Change Your Life Forever*, 22.
[166] Ibid, 109.

Epilogue

John Harper's words are reflections of the faith he lived out and died by, as he saw with compassion the hundreds dying around him in the North Atlantic before he, too, met his own demise. His words also reflect the lovely Countess of Rothes, who looked upon humanity with a similar, supernatural compassion that goes beyond all demographic particulars of gender, class, race, beliefs, and reputation.

Adorning the west wall of St. Mary's Church in Fairford reads a plaque in honor of Noël's legacy: "Noëlle, Widow of the 19th Earl of Rothes, and Beloved Wife of Col. Claud Macfie D.S.O. of Fayre Court, Fairford, At Rest 12 Sept 1956. Holiness is an infinite compassion for others. Greatness is to take the common things of life and walk truly among them. Happiness is a great love and much serving."[167]

May we all strive to "row" our lives with the same spirit Noël Leslie Macfie, Countess of Rothes did; for the types of ships Noël rowed with her legacy of love, justice, and unity are the only truly unsinkable ones.

---

167 June Lewis-Jones, *Around Fairford: Through Time* (Gloucestershire: Amberley Publishing, 2011), 37.

Bibliography

Adams, Moody. *The Titanic's Last Hero: A Startling True Story That Can Change Your Life Forever.* Belfast: Ambassador International, 2012.

American Red Cross Mississippi. "About Us: The Beginning of the Red Cross." *American Red Cross Mississippi.* Accessed November 2, 2023. https://www.redcross.org.ms/about-us/beginning-red-cross.

Arnold, Matthew. "Lines Written in Kensington Gardens." Poetry Foundation. https://www.poetryfoundation.org/poems/43593/lines-written-in-kensington-gardens, 1852.

Arnstein, Walter. "Queen Victoria and the Challenge of Roman Catholicism." *The Historian* 58. No. 2 (1996): 295-314. Accessed January 1, 2024. https://www.jstor.org/stable/24452277.

"Asleep in the Cradle of the Deep While Civilized World is Mourning." *The Daily Gate City.* April 21, 1912. https://www.newspapers.com/image/328430903/?match=1&terms=%22Asleep%20in%20the%20Cradle%20of%20the%20Deep%22.

"Atlantic History." *Schooner-Atlantic.* Accessed January 17, 2024. https://www.schooner-atlantic.com/atlantic-history.html.

Baird, Julia. *Victoria: The Queen: An Intimate Biography of the Woman Who Ruled an Empire.* New York: Random House, 2016.

Bancroft, James W. *The Titanic Disaster: Omens, Mysteries, and Misfortunes of the Doomed Liner.* Barnsley: Frontline Books, 2023.

Baumann, Sarah. "The Musicians of the *Titanic.*" One Day Creative. Last modified April 13, 2021. https://onedaycreative.com/the-musicians-of-the-titanic.

Beesley, Lawrence. *The Loss of the S.S. Titanic: Its Story and Its Lessons.* Boston: Mariner Books, 2000.

Behe, George. *Voices from the Carpathia: Rescuing RMS Titanic,* Gloucestershire: The History Press, 2015.

Beresford, Jack. "The Story of *RMS Carpathia*: 12 Incredible Facts About the Ship that Saved *Titanic*'s Survivors." *The Irish Post.* April 14, 2021. https://www.irishpost.com/life-style/rms-carpathia-12-facts-titanics-rescue-165987.

"Betrothal of a Countess." *Cheltenham Chronicle and Gloucestershire Graphic.* December 24, 1927. https://www.newspapers.com/image/786270108/?match=1&terms=rothes.

Bigham, Randy Bryan. "A Matter of Course: *Titanic*'s Plucky Little Countess." *Encyclopedia-Titanica.* Accessed January 10, 2023. https://www.encyclopedia-titanica.org/countess.html.

Blackwood, William. *The New Statistical Account of Scotland, Volume 10.* Edinburgh: William Blackwood & Sons, 1836.

Bracken, Robert L. "The Mystery of Rhoda Abbott Revealed." *Encyclopedia-Titanica.* Last modified June 7, 2004. https://www.encyclopedia-titanica.org/rhoda-abbott.html.

"Bremen Plowed Through Bodies." *The San Francisco Call and Post* (San Francisco, California) April 25, 1912. https://www.newspapers.com/

image/80851571/?match=1&terms=%22Women%20fainted%20in%20hysterics%20at%20the%20horror%20scene%22.

Brengle, W.D. "The Lost 'Atlantic.'" *The Ilfracombe Chronicle & North Devon News* (Ilfracombe, Devon, England), June 7, 1873. https://www.newspapers.com/image/797180654/?match=1&terms=%22While%20men%20to%20thee%20their%20fault%20allege%22.

Butcher, Tim. *The Trigger: Hunting the Assassin Who Brought the World to War.* New York: Grove Press, 2014.

Butler, Daniel Allen. *The Other Side of the Night: The Carpathia, The Californian, and the Night Titanic was Lost.* Havertown: Casemate, 2009.

Butler, Daniel Allen. *Unsinkable.* Boston: Da Capo Press, 2012.

Carter, William. "Requiem for *Titanic's* Dead." *The Rutland Herald.* April 22, 1912. https://www.newspapers.com/image/533741328/?match=1&terms=%22The%20floods%20have%20lifted%22.

Cherry, Gladys. "A Remarkable Letter." *The Daily Telegraph.* May 27, 1912. https://www.newspapers.com/image/818671595/?match=1&terms=%22I%20feel%20I%20must%20write%20and%20tell%20you%20how%22.

"Countess of Rothes Here After *Titanic* Experience." *The Los Angeles Daily Times.* May 16, 1912. https://www.newspapers.com/image/380257771/?terms=%22I%20was%20glad%20beyond%20expression%20to%20see%20my%20husband%22.

Countess of Rothes. "Silent Hour." *The Central Baptist.* May 12, 1910. https://www.newspapers.com/image/519421509/?match=1&terms=%22silent%20hour%22.

"The Countess Who Became Heroine of the *Titanic.*" *Western Daily Press.* January 30, 1998. https://www.newspapers.com/image/9219

36192/?match=1&terms=%22Like%20an%20earthquake%20or%20a%20distant%20battle%22.

"Death of King Edward: World Wide Sorrow." *Shepton Mallet Journal*. May 13, 1910. https://www.newspapers.com/image/806233848/?match=1&terms=%22Death%20of%20King%20Edward%22.

"Death of Mr. T. Dyer-Edwardes." *The Citizen*. February 12, 1926. https://www.newspapers.com/image/792093987/?match=1&terms=edwardes.

"Deaths." *The Citizen*. April 5, 1947. https://www.newspapers.com/image/792863190/?match=1&terms=Clementina

"The Earl of Rothes." *The Gloucestershire Echo*. March 30, 1927. https://www.newspapers.com/image/798744542/?match=1&terms=%22The%20Earl%20of%20Rothes%22.

"Echoes of Great Disaster." *The Kingston Daily Standard*. October 21, 1913. https://www.newspapers.com/image/785903039/?match=1&terms=%22Titanic%22.

"The English Church Union: Meeting in Gloucester." *The Gloucester Journal*. May 4, 1912. https://www.newspapers.com/image/792539756/?match=1&terms=%22Gloucester%20desires%20to%20proffer%20its%20deep%20sympathy%20with%20its%20late%20chairman%22.

"English Press Pays Tribute to Heroes." *The Buffalo News*. April 20, 1912. https://www.newspapers.com/image/352613324/?match=1&terms=%22All%20appeals%20are%20meeting%20with%20generous%20response%22.

Father Fabian. "The Countess Who Became Heroine of the *Titanic*." *Western Daily Press*. January 30, 1998. https://www.newspapers.

com/image/921936192/?match=1&terms=%22Like%20an%20 earthquake%20or%20a%20distant%20battle%22.

Fielding, Jenni. "How Much was a Ticket on the *Titanic?*" *Cruise Mummy*. Last modified February 20, 2024. https://www.cruise-mummy.co.uk/titanic-ticket-prices.

Franklin, Philip Albright. "Absolutely Unsinkable." *Binghamton Press and Leader*. April 15, 1912. https://www.newspapers.com/image/25251 1742/?match=1&terms=%22Franklin%22%20and%20%22Titanic%22.

Franklin, Philip Albright. *Messenger-Inquirer*. April 4, 2012. https:// www.newspapers.com/image/456357308/?match=1&terms=%22Th ere%20is%20no%20danger%20that%20Titanic%20will%20sink%22.

Franklin, Philip Albright. "Passengers of *Titanic* in Crash with Iceberg, Safe on Other Vessels." *Evening Star*. April 15, 1912. https://www.news-papers.com/image/331611150/?match=1&terms=%22gotten%20off%20 all%20the%20messages%20she%20wanted%20to%20send%22.

Franklin, Philip Albright. "Says Vessel is Unsinkable." *The Evening Star*. April 15, 1912. https://www.newspapers.com/image/331610978/ ?match=1&terms=%22We%20place%20absolute%20confidence%20 in%20the%20Titanic%22.

"Fraserburgh, 1919: A Capsized Crew in a Courageous Community." *Lifeboats RNLI 200*. April 25, 2019. https://rnli.org/magazine/ magazine-featured-list/2019/april/fraserburgh-capsized-crew.

Gloucestershire Echo, The. July 17, 1915. https://www.newspapers.com/ image/798684703/?match=1&terms=titanic.

Gracie, Archibald. *The Truth About Titanic*. New York: Mitchell Kennerley, 1913.

Havner, Vance. *The Vance Havner Quotebook.* Ed. Dennis J. Hester. Michigan: Baker Publishing Group, 1986.

"Heroic Conduct of Women Survivors." *The Daily Telegraph.* April 22, 1912. https://www.newspapers.com/image/818665953/?terms=%22Her%20boat%20was%20likewise%20undermanned%22.

"Horror of the Chase of the Phantom Light." *The Arkansas Gazette.* April 26, 1912. https://www.newspapers.com/image/138384366/?terms=%22whole%20attitude%20was%20one%20of%20great%20calmness%20and%20courage%22.

"How Many People Were on the *Titanic*? Here are Some Numbers." *History on the Net.* Accessed October 4, 2023. https://www.historyonthenet.com/how-many-people-were-on-the-titanic.

Hutchings, David and Richard de Kerbrech. *RMS Titanic Manual: 1909-1912 (Olympic Class) Owners' Workshop Manual.* Minnesota: Zenith Press, 2011.

"Iceberg Alley: Newfoundland and Labrador." *Atlas Obscura.* Last modified June 14, 2019. https://www.atlasobscura.com/places/iceberg-alley.

"Injured in *Titanic* Dream." *Portage Daily Register.* April 25, 1912. https://www.newspapers.com/image/611966031/?match=1&terms=%22Injured%20in%20Titanic%20Dream%22.

Jones, Ellen. "*Titanic*: Unlikely Friendship in Lifeboat Eight." *BBC News.* April 14, 2012. https://www.bbc.co.uk/news/uk-england-17583924.

Jones, Tom. "Countess of Rothes' Story: Her Ladyship in Charge of a Boat." *Gloucestershire Chronicle.* April 27, 1912. https://www.

newspapers.com/image/793131796/?match=1&terms=%22Her%20 Ladyship%20in%20Charge%20of%20a%20Boat%22.

Jones, Tom. "Heroic Conduct of Women." *Huddersfield Daily Examiner.* April 22, 1912. https://www.newspapers.com/image/815475566/?match=1&terms=%22Heroic%20Conduct%20of%20Women%22.

Jones, Tom. "Letter to Countess." *Encyclopedia-Titanica.* Accessed January 18, 2024. https://www.encyclopedia-titanica.org/titanic-survivor/thomas-william-jones.html.

Kaye, Elizabeth. *Lifeboat No. 8: An Untold Tale of Love, Loss, and Surviving the Titanic.* La Jolla, CA: The Sager Group LLC, 2018.

Kopstein, Jack. "The Valiant Musicians: Wallace Hartley and the *Titanic* Ship's Orchestra." *World Military Bands: The Heritage of Military Bands.* Accessed October 9, 2023. https://archive.ph/20130105160913/http://www.worldmilitarybands.com/the-valiant-musicians.

Kovach, Kathy. "Two Heroines of the *Titanic.*" *Heroes, Heroines, & History.* Last modified October 12, 2019. https://www.hhhistory.com/2019/10/two-heroines-of-titanic.html?m=1.

"Lady Rothes: The *Titanic*'s Heroine." *Nobility.org.* Last modified June 30, 2016. https://nobility.org/2016/06/lady-rothes-titanics-heroine.

"The Latest." *The Cobar Herald.* April 23, 1912. https://www.newspapers.com/image/969550216/?match=1&terms=%22she%20found%20the%20men%20could%20not%20row%22.

"The Launch of the *Olympic*: The Biggest Ship Afloat." *The Derby Daily Telegraph.* October 21, 1910. https://www.newspapers.com/image/790860002/?terms=%22The%20sun%20shone%20brilliantly%20on%20this%20latest%20enterprise%22.

Lauriat, Charles E. *The Lusitania's Last Voyage: Being a Narrative of the Torpedoing and Sinking of the R.M.S. Lusitania by a German Submarine off the Irish Coast.* United States: Undersea Publishing, 2020.

"The Leslie Story." *Clan Leslie Trust.* Accessed January 14, 2024. https://clanleslietrust.org/the-leslie-story.

Lewis-Jones, June. *Around Fairford: Through Time.* Gloucestershire: Amberley Publishing, 2011.

Lightoller, Charles. *Titanic and Other Ships*, Benediction Classics, 2010.

Lindsay, Muriel C. "The Countess and the Captain." *The Newcastle Weekly Chronicle.* November 2, 1912. https://www.newspapers.com/image/815081116/?match=1&terms=%22The%20Countess%20and%20the%20Captain%22.

"Local Commissions." *The Gloucester Journal.* December 22, 1917. https://www.newspapers.com/image/793739866/?match=1&terms=%22earl%20of%20rothes%22.

"London Incidents: Memorial Service at St. Paul's Cathedral." *The Western Times.* April 20, 1912. https://www.newspapers.com/image/816846818/?match=1&terms=%22London%20Incidents%22.

"Lord Rothes Puts His Estate in Scotland on the Market." *The Washington Post.* July 19, 1919. https://www.newspapers.com/image/31539121/?match=1&terms=%22lord%20rothes%20puts%20his%20estate%20in%20scotland%22.

Lord, Walter. *A Night to Remember.* London: R&W Holt, 1955.

"Lucy Noëlle Martha Dyer-Edwardes." The Peerage. Accessed November 7, 2023, https://www.thepeerage.com/p8538.htm#i85377.

"Malcolm George Dyer-Edwardes Leslie, 20th Earl of Rothes." The Peerage. Accessed November 8, 2023, https://www.thepeerage.com/p8539.htm#i85382.

Medhurst, Simon. *Titanic: Day by Day*. Barnsley: Pen and Sword History, 2022.

"A Mixed Ancestry." *Pittsburgh Post-Gazette*. March 14, 1900. https://www.newspapers.com/image/85571192/?match=1&terms=%22Lady%20Henrietta%20Leslie%22.

Mize, Douglas W. "As *Titanic* Sank, He Pleaded, 'Believe in the Lord Jesus!'" *Baptist Press*, April 13, 2012. https://www.baptistpress.com/resource-library/news/as-titanic-sank-he-pleaded-believe-in-the-lord-jesus.

"Mr. T Dyer-Edwardes' Thank-Offering." *The Gloucester Journal*. August 14, 1915. https://www.newspapers.com/image/792520513/?match=1&terms=%22thank-offering%22.

Newman, John Henry. *Apologia Pro Vita Sua: Being a Reply to a Pamphlet Entitled 'What, Then, Does Dr. Newman Mean?'* London: Longman, Green, Longman, Roberts, and Green, 1864.

Newman, John Henry. "Letters and Correspondence 1833 – Sicily: To F. Rogers, Esq.," *Newman Reader*. Last modified June 5, 1833, https://www.newmanreader.org/biography/mozley/volume1/file9.html.

Newman, John Henry. *Lead, Kindly Light*. 1833. Newman University. Accessed November 19, 2023. https://www.cardinaljohnhenrynewman.com/lead-kindly-light.

New-York Tribune. 1904. https://www.newspapers.com/image/4687 11770/?match=1&terms=%22Originally%20it%20formed%20an%20 immense%20quadrangle%22.

"Norman Evelyn Leslie, 19th Earl of Rothes." The Peerage. Accessed November 7, 2023. https://www.thepeerage.com/p8538.htm#i85377.

"Notes of the Day." *Devon and Exeter Gazette.* April 12, 1912. https://www.newspapers.com/image/791439955/?match=1&terms=%2 2to%20meet%20the%20Earl%20of%20Rothes%22.

Olson, Donald W., Russell L. Doescher, and Roger W. Sinnott. "Rare Astronomical Confluence: Did the Moon Sink the *Titanic?*" *Sky and Telescope.* April 2012. https://skyandtelescope.org/wp-content/uploads/Titanic+layout.pdf.

Paz, Denis G. *Popular Anti-Catholicism in Mid-Victorian England.* Stanford: Stanford University Press, 1992.

"Prinknash Park: Owner's Offer Not Accepted by Bishop Gloucester." *The Citizen.* January 2, 1926. https://www.newspapers.com/image/7 92089032/?match=1&terms=%22Bishop%20of%20Gloucester%22.

Robertson, Morgan. *The Wreck of the Titan.* Virginia: Wilder Publications, Inc., 1898.

"A Romantic Isle." *The Manchester Evening News.* September 29, 1928. https://www.newspapers.com/image/937825394/?match=1&terms =%22Prinknash%20Park%22.

Russell, Gareth. *The Ship of Dreams: The Sinking of the Titanic and the End of the Edwardian Era.* New York: Atria Books, 2019.

Bibliography

"Service Over Each of the 116 Bodies Buried at Sea." *St. Louis Post Dispatch.* May 1, 1912. https://www.newspapers.com/image/138924026/?match=1&terms=%22Mackay-Bennett%22.

"Shipwreck: An Awful Record!" *The Boston Globe.* April 2, 1873. https://www.newspapers.com/image/428970028/?match=1&terms=%22an%20awful%20record%22.

Slathersome, Percival. "'Just Missed It' Club Might Have Sunk *Titanic* at Dock." *The Spokane Press.* April 22, 1912. https://www.newspapers.com/image/932287715/?match=1&terms=%22Percival%20Slathersome%22.

"Snapshots at Social Leaders." *The Washington Post.* April 25, 1912. https://www.newspapers.com/image/28899455/?match=1&terms=%22Perhaps%20she%20recalled%20the%20family%20motto%22.

"Social and Personal." *Glasgow Herald.* April 20, 1900. https://www.newspapers.com/image/409214828/?match=1&terms=rothes.

"The Story of an Old Timer: Wireless Ship Act." *National Institute of Standards and Technology U.S. Department of Commerce.* Accessed December 28, 2023. https://www.nist.gov/pml/nbsnist-radio-stations-story-old-timer/story-old-timer-navy/story-old-timer-wireless-ship-act.

"Sunken Liner $7,500,000 Palace." *The New York Times.* April 16, 1912. https://www.newspapers.com/image/26040649/?match=1&terms=Sunken%20Liner%20%247%2C500%2C000%20Palace.

"A Sword Thrust out of the Deep." *The Daily Republican.* April 19, 1912. https://www.newspapers.com/image/549342535/?match=1&terms=%22A%20Sword%20Thrust%20out%20of%20the%20Deep%22.

"Thomas William Jones: *RMS Titanic* Able Seaman." *Encyclopedia-Titanica*. Accessed November 14, 2023. https://www.encyclopedia-titanica.org/titanic-survivor/thomas-william-jones.html.

"The *Titanic*." Smithsonian Institution. Accessed November 10, 2023. https://www.si.edu/spotlight/titanic#:~:text=The%20Titanic%20was%20a%20White%20Star%20Line%20steamship,Ireland%2C%20at%20a%20reported%20cost%20of%20%247.5%20million.

"*Titanic* Hearing." *Boston Evening Transcript*. April 27, 1912. https://www.newspapers.com/image/735684965/?match=1&terms=%22most%20unwise%22.

"*Titanic* in Peril on Leaving Port." *The New York Times*. April 11, 1912. https://www.newspapers.com/image/20639997/?match=1&terms=%22Titanic%20in%20Peril%20on%20Leaving%20Port%22.

"*Titanic*'s Captain Skipper 40 Years." *Fall River Evening News*. April 16, 1912. https://www.newspapers.com/image/590545495/?match=1&terms=%22Modern%20shipbuilding%20has%20gone%20beyond%20that%22.

Tute, Warren. *Atlantic Conquest: The Men and Ships of the Glorious Age of Steam*. Boston: Little Brown Publishers, 1962.

"Two Heroes in 'Wireless' Room." *The Daily Mirror*. April 20, 1912. https://www.newspapers.com/image/789729135/?match=1&terms=%22I%20went%20out%20on%20deck%20and%20looked%20around%22.

Uglow, Nicholas, Tom Addyman, and John Lowrey. "The Archaeology and Conservation of the Country House: Leslie House and Kinross Home." *Architectural Heritage XXIII* (2012): 163-178. Accessed December

19, 2023. https://www.research.ed.ac.uk/en/publications/the-archaeology-and-conservation-of-the-country-house-leslie-hous.

United States Senate Inquiry, Day 7. *Titanic Inquiry Project*. Accessed January 20, 2024. https://www.titanicinquiry.org/USInq/AmInq07Jones01.php.

"Vessel Near *Titanic?*" *The Washington Post*. April 22, 1912. https://www.newspapers.com/image/28898026/?match=1&terms=%22Miss%20Gladys%20Cherry%22.

Wade, Wyn Craig. *The Titanic: Disaster of the Century*. New York: Skyhorse, 2012.

Warrender, Claire. "Leslie House: Restoration Finally Under Way at the Home of *Titanic* Heroine." *The Courier Evening Telegraph*. September 9, 2021. https://www.thecourier.co.uk/fp/news/fife/2517314/leslie-house-restoration-finally-under-way-at-the-home-of-titanic-heroine/.

Welsh, Anna Marie. *Heroes of the Titanic*. London: Tangerine Press, 2011.

"Women of the *Titanic*, The." *The New York Times*. April 21, 1912. https://www.newspapers.com/image/26042879/?match=1&terms=%22meeting%20the%20terrible%20ordeal%20so%20courageously%22.

About the Author

Dr. Lona Bailey is an award-winning Golden Age of Hollywood researcher and writer of *Uncredited: The Life and Career of Actress Virginia Gregg, Voice of Villainy: The Betty Lou Gerson Story, Mrs. Radio: The Cathy Lewis Story,* and *Some Small Nobility: The Biography of Joan Banks Lovejoy.* Dr. Bailey's *Voice of Villainy* biography was a finalist in the International Book Awards for 2023 and won the Gold Medal Award in the Dan Poynter's Global Ebook Awards Contest of 2023. Dr. Bailey has been featured on *The Wolfe Den Show,* in *Film Daily,* and in *The Los Angeles Tribune.*

Coming Soon

That's the Way She Became Alice Nelson:
The Biography of The Brady Bunch's Ann B. Davis

Ambassador International's mission is to magnify the Lord Jesus Christ and promote His Gospel through the written word.

We believe through the publication of Christian literature, Jesus Christ and His Word will be exalted, believers will be strengthened in their walk with Him, and the lost will be directed to Jesus Christ as the only way of salvation.

For more information about AMBASSADOR INTERNATIONAL please visit:

www.ambassador-international.com
@AmbassadorIntl
www.facebook.com/AmbassadorIntl

Thank you for reading this book!

You make it possible for us to fulfill our mission, and we are grateful for your partnership.

To help further our mission, please consider leaving us a review on your social media, favorite retailer's website, Goodreads or Bookbub, or our website, and check out some of the books on the following page!

More from Ambassador International

During the time of the Raj in India, Amy Carmichael discovered a custom of the time in which children were 'married to gods' and so introduced to a life of prostitution. With a mixture of courage and heartbreak, she began to uncover the facts, sometimes under disguise, for the government. Against difficult circumstances, Amy and her colleagues provided a safe home for these children against awesomely difficult circumstances at Dohnavur in South India. Until her death in 1951, she devoted fifty years of her life to rescuing babies and children from dangerous backgrounds in India.

George Whitefield made five successful itinerant preaching tours throughout colonial New England, during which he was both appreciated and unwelcomed. Whitefield shook colonial New England, as a blessing to some and as a curse to others. *George Whitefield's Ministry*, written by Kenneth Lawson, is a travelogue of Whitefield's incessant activities to the Puritan and post-Puritan communities.

In *Worldchangers*, challenge your faith as you meet men and women from around the world who turned some of the darkest moments of history into transforming opportunities. Experience the true stories of Christians who lived the adventure of saying yes to a faithful God and be transported to unforgettable moments when ordinary people trusted God for things that seemed impossible and, as a result, changed the world for the better.

www.ingramcontent.com/pod-product-compliance
Lightning Source LLC
Chambersburg PA
CBHW060519090426
42735CB00011B/2295